Tempus ORAL HISTORY *Series*

Rochdale
voices

The Sacred Heart Whit Walk, c. 1955.

Tempus ORAL HISTORY *Series*

Rochdale
voices

Compiled by
Helen Caffrey

TEMPUS

First published 2000
Copyright © Helen Caffrey, 2000

Tempus Publishing Limited
The Mill, Brimscombe Port,
Stroud, Gloucestershire, GL5 2QG

ISBN 0 7524 1651 0

Typesetting and origination by
Tempus Publishing Limited
Printed in Great Britain by
Midway Clark Printing, Wiltshire

Brownies and Guides at St Edmund's church in the mid-1930s.

Contents

Three generations: Elsie Schofield (centre) with her mother and daughter Muriel on a seaside holiday.

Introduction

This book grew out of a college history class. Some of the members have met together for twenty years to discuss local and social history; students are in their seventies, eighties and nineties. When I started teaching the class I found that I talked about a topic and they gave me the local and particular details. I tried to take down notes, then realized their voices should be recorded. I spoke to my friends in museums, libraries and the sound archive. When a new term started I proposed a book to the class, and together we drew up a list of topics. Sometimes each person spoke in turn, often a group shared their experiences, and so some passages in this book were heard as conversation. A few new contributors responded to an enquiry in the *Rochdale Observer*, especially describing their work and memories of former traditions.

    This is not a definitive history of Rochdale, nor is it everyone's experience here in the period roughly from the 1920s to the 1950s. It is, however, real and individual. Some memories go back further where they incorporate those of parents and other relatives. We didn't talk about the good old days or bad old days, but tried to see our own experience within a framework of change over a generation. Soon it will be time for the next generation of voices. What will change and what stay the same? Will the coming of motor vehicles, television and the war (at the end of our period) be seen as a turning-point, the end of an era? Perhaps the pace of change will seem to accelerate while local differences diminish. But I think many essentials will continue: children's play, families and friendship, appreciation and observation of local places,

Traditional Rochdale: Blackwater Street by St Mary's Gate, near the college where we met to produce this book.

customs and peculiarities. So, reader, when you listen to our 'Voices', attend to your own. Perhaps our book will encourage you too to record your local memories.

As all the material here, except for the reminiscences of the maypole, was transcribed from tape-recordings, so it preserves the cadence of speech and some of the style of conversation. Some words here evoke a particular period – 'nutty slack' and 'snook'. Other descriptions may be familiar, or represent variations, by other names, as in the games played – 'jigger', 'cappie' and 'trinnell'. The chapter on work records weaving, nursing and engineering, among other occupations, which have experienced change in attitudes and practice as well as in economic trends. And an area of our lives, changed beyond return but still taking much of our time, is shopping – where did we go for our coffee, bacon and biscuits? While retracing local haunts and delights we recall a plethora of picture-palaces, and the dance floor and bobby horses at Hollingworth Lake. For the rest, you must read it for yourselves, till the coda, where our last Voice challenges us: can we look back truly with nostalgia tempered by understanding?

Helen Caffrey
March 2000

Compiler Helen Caffrey in 1951, aged two and a half.

Acknowledgements

Rochdale Voices: Jim Barham, Ron Burrows, Barbara Eldred, Pamela Hutchinson, Sheila Jones, Ronnie Kershaw, Alan Mills, Jean Roberts, Joan Thomson, Margaret Turner, Kath Ward, Anon, and other supporting Voices. Maypole memories: E. Seddon, J. Hall, H. Wolfenden, M. Cairns, E. Halliday, V. Wilson.

I should like to acknowledge the support and encouragement of Rochdale Museum Service, especially Debbie Walker; the Local Studies Library for their help with illustrations; former colleagues and past teachers of the local history class at Hopwood Hall College; the North West Sound Archive for agreeing to store the tapes as an archive; Rochdale Photographic Society; and many unheard local people for whom we are in some sort a voice.

CHAPTER 1

Games We Played

No traffic on the roads: Ashfield Road, 1925.

Games for Every Day

These things seemed to go by rote. Nobody knew just when they were coming in, there was no set calendar. Call it folklore if you like, but now whips and tops were in, then skipping-ropes came out.

Kath Ward

Marbles

With the lads particularly it was hide-and-seek, and marbles. We played marbles all the way to school and back – playing got you to school – there was no traffic on the roads of course, so we played at the side of the roads.

Alan Mills

Jigger

Sometimes fights started. You had a team say of boys, one called the 'belly-stopper' with his back to the wall. The first man of the team bent down and the others followed behind and there was a line with their backs bent down. The team that was jumping came up, jumped as far as they could while the ones underneath tried to shake them off. If someone jumped on and his foot touched the floor it was his turn. You could appeal to the belly-stopper. The leader would hold one finger up and the others had to guess which finger it was – dick, prick, kalamanker, jack and little tom. It was a rough game.

Ronnie Kershaw

Peggy and Cappie

There was 'peggy', a little shaped piece of wood and you had to hit it and run. You hit it with the peggy stick as far as you could, then you'd look at your opponent and try to weigh up how many strides – just too much and he had to jump it out and if he did it within that number it counted to him

Some things never change: childrens' games at Middleton around 1900, with the previous generation playing the games Ronnie describes here.

Ronnie, sedately posed with his father, c. 1910.

and if he failed it counted to you, so you had to make a nice judgement. I once got done with that because my opponent counted it over a wall so I gave him a task of so many strides but he jumped over the wall – that was cheating!

Ronnie Kershaw

Hoops

Some were wood and some were iron. The iron ones had a thing you held with a little hook on it so you could run along and keep control of it – you used to go for miles. It was as good as a bicycle. The girls mainly had the wooden ones.

Ronnie Kershaw

Ball Games

Biff-bat was a little tiny ball on elastic and you hit it – it was attached to the bat. There was battledore and shuttlecock, like a poor man's badminton. My parents used to play.

The Group

Whips and Tops

We spent a lot of time making the tops beautiful with coloured chalks, and if it rubbed off we put it on again in blues and reds.

There were different shapes – some that were a bit like a carrot, others called 'window breakers', with a stem and top like a darning-mushroom – you had to

keep up with them – and short, stubby ones as well.

The whip was strong string, or leather if you could afford it, and when the top swung round all the colours mixed up.

Jean Roberts, Barbara Eldred

'Seen you, Seen You'

In 'kick the can' you'd all run away and hide. Somebody was on and he'd kick the can as far as he could. Then you had to creep back without being seen. You'd shout, 'Seen you, seen you' till one was left who hadn't been seen – we enjoyed it.

Ron Burrows

Counting

We used to play 'What time is it Mr Wolf?' Of course we always used to pick who was on by doing 'One potato, two potato', till my brother sussed out how to start, so he was never the one who was on!

Anon

A Chasing Game

Another was 'trinnell', a chasing game. You'd be chasing everyone and the one you collared had to join the line, so you'd end up with about half a dozen people running around and twenty of you in a line. You'd run round to try and enclose them.

Ronnie Kershaw

Paved streets: Edenfield Road with tramlines and gas lamp.

Cycling in the Mill

When my mother worked at the mill, I had a little two-wheeler bike and I used to ride my bike up to the mill. Then I used to be riding my bike up and down the alleys of the mill. Talk about safety, there was no safety at all in those days.

Joan Thomson

Your Duck's Off

'Duckstones' – Gracie Fields used to call out in the middle of a song 'Your duck's off' – we used to play regularly. You had a flat stone and everyone picked a stone he could chuck and put it on it and that was the duck. The rest were behind the line and threw at it. If they missed they had to try and recover their duck and get back. He could come and tap you and then it was your turn to have it. Of course you chased around, and if your pals were throwing and knocked it off, they shouted, 'Your duck's off' so he couldn't 'tig' you. You had to go back and put it on and everyone ran behind the baseline.

Ron Burrows, Ronnie Kershaw

Change

Some of these games might have died out when streets became Tarmacked not paved. You couldn't play on top of it like smooth flags. Of course you could play on the street and never see a vehicle for an hour or two and you had lamp-posts for wickets in cricket.

Alan Mills

13

Little Muriel Schofield with her mother Elsie, grandmother, and favourite doll.

Imagination

You could make any amount of things out of little pegs, like cowboys with little paper hats, colour their faces and make little jackets for them and then you'd be the cowboy.

Ron Burrows

Handwork

The girls had those milk bottle tops. Where they now have the covering on top, they had a wider neck and a card disc. There was a hole in the middle that you pushed in to get the disc out and of course you kept the discs and put wool round, often in blanket stitch and you joined on a number of them and made a little mat. That was an occupation for a winter's day when you couldn't go out.

The Group

Snakes and Beetles!

We played ludo, snakes and ladders, snap, donkey, those sort of games. We collected things in matchboxes – beetles and ladybirds, stamps.

The Group

Collecting

All the lads had cigarette cards of course. You used to line them up on a wall and flick your card at them and that would tell you who had it. You didn't use your best cards for that. Then you had skimming, when you tried to lay your card on the others.

There was a line-up of cards which took the place of cigarette cards – 'play-ups' we used to call them. All the football teams were on them and each one said, 'Play Up Rochdale' or 'Play Up Chelsea', something like that. You tried to collect your favourite teams, but you had to buy those. Every newsagent's shop had a little bag of play-ups, and of course you always got something you didn't want and then you swapped them.

Ron Burows

Quiet games: John and Peter playing in 1945.

Swapping Scraps

Then you collected scraps. You could buy them in those days. They were little pictures, a penny plain and twopence coloured, and you had a scrap-book and stuck your best ones in, but you could do quite a good trade swapping them with other people, you know, this one and that one, and that's worth two of these. They were common, you could buy a bag full, or loose, from the local paper shop.

Ron Burrows

Cutting and Sticking

Ron with his elder brother. This photograph 'Happy as Sandboys' won their father a guinea prize from the Daily Dispatch *in the late 1920s.*

You could get cutting-out sheets too. There were soldiers, forts and houses and you had to cut them out very carefully and stick them together. You could get some to make roundabouts, make a chute at the top and fill it with dry sand and when it came down the roundabout went round. You had to be older to do that and it kept you going many a night. Glue wasn't all that good in those days and you had to sit there for ages holding the edges until the glue dried.

Ron Burrows

Working Models

I was really lucky. The lad next door was getting into his late teens and losing his interest in Meccano. He passed this huge box onto us and we all used to get together building towers, bridges, cranes – they all had to work.

My brother-in-law used to make model ships when he was a lad and he fastened elastic on them and fired the guns from the boat. The skirting-board in the house where they lived still has holes in it where he used to fire his torpedo!

Ron Burrows

A Playground Game

We used to sing, 'The good ship sailed on the ally-ally-o, on the fourteenth of September'. You had a long line of people and you all wound through – and then the teacher came and blew the whistle to go in. I don't know why it was that particular date; someone thought it was the opening of the Manchester Ship Canal, but it wasn't.

Kath Ward, Ronnie Kershaw

Party Games

At chapel there was a game we always played at our Christmas parties. We have a person who lies down 'Roger is dead', the rest go round in a circle, 'the apple tree grows over his head, heigh-ho the apples fell down, the apples fell down all over his head, then came a poor woman a-picking them up, Roger got up and he gave her a thump, and the poor old woman went hippety-hop.' When you're there and all doing it, it comes back to you. That was one we always used to do; there's always been a tradition of doing it.

Kath Ward

CHAPTER 2

How We Lived

The Old Boat Inn on Belfield Road, known locally as 'Uncle Tom's Cabin', seen through the smog. A housing estate now stands on this site.

Home

We did our cooking in the living-room. We had an iron fireplace with an oven and a boiler, but the boiler was cracked so it was never used. We never had the job of carrying water from the living-room into the kitchen. If we wanted water in quantity we used the gas boiler that we had for washing clothes. The lights were gaslights and we had a table with two gas jets for heating milk or cooking vegetables. Cooking meat had to be done in the fire oven, and bread – that was done on Friday afternoon. Our tin bath hung in the pantry and it was brought out into the kitchen. We had no fireplace in the kitchen but we had a gas boiler so the water could heat and be ladled out with a lading-can. I never noticed feeling cold.

Anon

A New Sink

Kitchenwise we didn't have the old slop-stone, we had the porcelain – they call it a Belfast sink now. My mother was always poorly from when I was about eleven, and I think my dad got one of the first washing-machines. It stood in the corner with the legs stuck out in the way. It had an agitator and the wringer on top. It did its job well. Then we had a gas boiler next to it and an electric oven, so really I suppose we weren't so old-fashioned as regards some of them. We had electric light all through and a little gas fire in the bedroom. I remember once or twice I was poorly in the back bedroom and it was so warm to go to sleep with this lovely glow, lovely and warm.

We had a cellar where my dad used to put eggs down in a crock, the tall sort, with isinglass. It was a coal-cellar but down by the steps and just to the right was a stone slab so milk and butter and things were kept down there. The cellar steps had to be washed, scrubbed and stoned. When our mum was in bed a lot I did it now and then.

When I was courting my husband, I went up and saw their kitchen. His father was a bit behind the times and had a slop-stone, but when I started visiting they had a sink put in!

Jean Roberts

Sunday Best

These ranges with the boiler and oven were made of steel and if you took a pride in them you had to blacklead them quite regularly. Some of them had a steel trim on top where the flues went. They weren't stainless steel like you think of today but steel that had to be polished. I can remember something like a small square of chain-mail with a lining and you used this to buff it up. At my grandmother's the hearth had a kind of tin plate and a fender and if you were very house-proud you changed them on a Sunday. You had a special hearthrug on Sunday as well, a newer one that you didn't use every day when you were slopping water. They went down on a Saturday night and I suppose came up on a Sunday night. I remember having stockings on table legs at my grandmother's, old stockings that you fastened round your table legs to protect them and then they came off on a Sunday.

I can remember seeing my dad doing peg rugs with one of these little hooks. You cut all the rags up and made nice little patterns as you went along. You were all working together.

Kath Ward

The Range

My mother didn't blacklead her range. She varnished it with black Wadicor's varnish. Oh, she was very house-proud. She used the varnish to save her energy.

Anon

Storage Space

Our stairs went up from the back door, so as you came from the living-room into the kitchen there was a door here into the pantry. We didn't have a cellar so there was a stone slab here. As the stairs went up they were bounded off. It was known as 'Klondike' – 'Oh, it's up on Klondike' they'd

Eating melons: Kath with her family and friends behind her home in Overt Street around 1930.

say if you wanted anything. I don't know if it was just common to our area. You found things there like a gold strike!

Kath Ward

Moor-enders

My grandfather was a moor-ender. They had rights over sections of the moor on a peppercorn rent. The whole family lived in the village around until some of them moved to Burnley when the mining ran out in Rochdale. His house had no running water nor any artificial light except candles. After the 1914 war my uncle came home full of modern ideas and he brought an Aladdin lamp that you pumped up so he had a bright light for the first time.

My uncle was very progressive and lived to be ninety-three. My aunt was quite a feature. She was blind and used to have to go down to the well and to Healey Stones, walking back with a fourteen-pound bag of flour on her head. She called it a 'poke'. She would walk from the Provident Store, up the hill, along the bottom and along the hillside to Mooredge. 'Blind Betty' she was called. She used to recognize your footsteps.

We lived a quarter of a mile away in a two-up two-down, and for a long time it didn't have a back door. You came through one room into the back room and there was no door to it. We had a range and a little wash-house so the bath was kept in the wash-house and brought in and put in front of the fire.

The fireplace had several bars and you could make lovely toast. You could put a teapot on the top to keep warm, and there was a little brass rail around and that had to

Ronnie's mother by the pigeon loft on a good drying day.

Resting after the day's work: Ronnie's father in 1930.

be polished too. My father was very handy and made a sort of toasting-fork that you could slide on the top bar and it hung down with hooks – an automatic toaster! Toasters nowadays don't make toast like you could make in front of the fire.

When you wanted to cook you had a cast-iron block you pulled out with a poker. Then you could shuffle the fire under the oven and when it was hot do your baking. When you put it back it didn't get hot but stayed warm – if you were going out you could put your scarf in to keep warm, but occasionally you forgot and they got burnt up.

On the other side was the water which you had to fill up with a lading-can. In fact, there used to be a chap just up here by the Pavilion who made lading-cans. You opened up the boiler, took out a lading-can full if you wanted to wash and took it to the slop-stone. We had an enamel basin as the slop-stone was solid stone. Then you filled the lading-can again because you always replaced what you used. Once every year it was emptied and whitewashed inside so the water was always clean water.

Ronnie Kershaw

Continuity

The house where I grew up was built of stone, with a vestibule into the front room. Then you walked through the front room to get into the back room. They called that room 'the house' because that's where everything was. The front room had a sofa and armchairs to match in a green pattern and some standing chairs. It was used at Christmas and on occasions; generally people stayed in the other room.

This house never changed. My grandparents had lived there and my aunt lived there from being born until she was eighty-nine.

A new fireplace was put in but not one thing was altered during her lifetime. There was a mangle with wooden rollers and these were eventually replaced with rubber ones. Lampshades went up when the electricity was brought in. The lavatory was in the backyard. When the wooden seat rotted she insisted on having another made which the joiner found a bit comical! She was a hardy old soul and had the bath in the kitchen but it must have been hard filling it. She didn't believe in

The men of the family: Barbara's grandfather Jim Proctor (back left) with his brothers.

having alterations as it would spoil the house for someone else.

Anon

Tippler Toilets

We had an outside toilet, a tippler. The water that flushed it came from the sink and the roof gutters. Ashworth put a lot of these tipplers in; brown ceramic they were. The water filled up and tipped automatically so it could be quite a surprise sometimes! If you were on the toilet you got the lot. The men used to come round to empty them. They did a really necessary job. They wore these great big leather aprons and used chloride of lime to combat the smells.

The Group

Modernization

Coming into the 1920s, Father had this idea of having a posh fireplace and so the old range came out, but there was still a back boiler and a washing-machine with a wringer on top. It clipped on and you had to turn it. Of course we didn't have a fridge, but under the stairs there was a slab for keeping things cool and we had a meat-safe in the yard.

Alan Mills

A Bathroom

In our house we were fortunate to have a bathroom. But it was rented, you see, and

the doctor me dad worked for, he had it put in. The others down the road hadn't.

Jean Roberts

Carpets

Carpets weren't fitted then. Every spring you took these carpets up and took them outside and batted them.

Pamela Hutchinson

Weekly Routine

Monday was washing day, and Thursday was baking day. Mother used to say, 'I'm not cooking a meal on Monday,' so it was always cold roast meat, then probably on Tuesday you'd have hash, potato pie on Thursday

The Group

Baking

The bread was kneaded in the mug and used to stand in front of the fire to rise. I love the shape of those things – they were earthenware with a yellow glaze inside, brown outside. I remember getting into trouble, poking my finger in the dough – I got clouted anyway!

Pamela Hutchinson, Ronnie Kershaw

Sunday Tea

Your parents' friends used to come and it was quite a tradition. You put out a tin of

Ronnie's family having tea on a fine day in the 1910s. Ronnie is in the centre of the group.

salmon and a jar of white pickles on the table.

There might be boiled ham and a tin of fruit with evaporated milk, usually a home-made cake and perhaps chocolate biscuits.

Kath Ward

A Bottle of Pop

We used to have a treat on Sunday, us kids. We had a big bottle of Tizer and it was the only time we were allowed pop. Mother said it was rubbish and rotted your teeth!

Sheila Jones

Like a Small Farm in a Town

My grandmother's kitchen in Derby had a shallow sink and at the side was a black wrought-iron pump to get the water – you had to be left-handed too. In the garden she grew everything. It was a long garden with all sorts of fruits: she made blackcurrant tea if you were poorly, and dandelion wine. Everything was kept in the cellar and there used to be explosions going off. They had hens and each member of the family – five girls and one boy – had their own chores to do. It was like running a little farm and yet it was a terraced-house. My mother used to collect the eggs.

There was a huge oven with a great big copper kettle on it and that had a tap on it. Grandmother used to say she put her corsets in the oven at night while it was cooling down.

I remember the horsehair dining-chairs with rounded, shiny seats – murder to sit on for little children with short dresses. Grandfather used to have his time of day when he'd lie on the *chaise longue* and cover his face. Everyone had to make themselves scarce!

No one seemed to own their homes in those days, they were all rented, so if you had any innovations of any sort you had to depend on your landlord. I remember when I was a little girl I was lifted up with a taper to light the gas. The lights over the fireplace were converted to electricity and they looked quite nice as they had these glass shaped bulbs in them. In our house we had a set boiler in the kitchen – that was a do on a Monday – it had a nice wooden top on it for the rest of the week. It stood in the corner, three-cornered with a brick front. When I was young the landlord installed a bathroom which had this massive geyser. It was very, very smelly and noisy, but I was an only one so it was a pretty quiet life – you weren't always queuing up for things.

Pamela Hutchinson

Gassed!

Those geysers had to fill with gas before they could ignite. A friend of mine collapsed when the room filled with gas.

Anon

Sleeping on a Rope

Along River Street and all that were doss-houses. They used to charge a penny a night and they'd go in and be under cover. They'd no beds or anything, they'd sleep on a rope, hang over it with it under the armpits. In the morning she'd come in and undo the rope and time was up. You could see down the windows into the cellars along Archer Street, and the tobacco smoke was coming out.

Jim Barham

Cold

I can remember being cold as a child, feeling cold, because you had to be immediately in front of the fire.

Anon

A new home in the 1920s, but Ronnie's neighbours thought he'd found a bomb when this petrol tank was found beneath the garden!

CHAPTER 3

Going to School

Girls' games at New Hey School, c. 1900.

Board School

Derby Street was a board school, it did you up till fourteen, but if you got through your eleven-plus you left then. I lived on Ashfield Road so it was a case of walking to school and walking back. It wasn't very far. We did writing, joining-up writing, times tables, and we did a little bit of sewing. We had this white canvas stuff with holes and you had what was known as floss; you just made cross-stitches and made it into a little purse. There was a little bit of art or maybe drawing with Miss Broadhurst or Miss Heywood. I didn't mind going to school.

Kath Ward

Getting Started

I was dying to go to school. What I thought it was going to be like I have no idea! When

I got there it can't have come up to my expectations because I used to cry all the time. I wasn't five I was only four and I made myself quite ill. People said to my mother, 'Oh, I should take her away because she's not five yet,' but my mother said, 'I'm not going through all this again, she'll have to stay.'

I remember the handwriting, three lines and you went half-way up for the small letters. At the end of the afternoon the teacher used to read a story, quite advanced things because I can remember *Mill on the Floss* and this was in elementary school.

Anon

Discipline

I was five and a half before I went to school. I was five in September and the parents thought it was no time to start school so I went in at Easter. I was desperately anxious to go to school because the lady next door kept saying, 'If they find out your father will go to prison.' Then my father took me and the girl next door to school and I liked it.

I could read – in fact they had me teaching other children and I can remember one of the boys teaching me to write. We had one teacher who sang on the wireless. We didn't have a wireless but she gave a recital in Champness Hall after we'd left Derby Street. We were invited and they gave me five tickets to sell to friends. She thought nothing of twamping the boys, she'd bend over them, and the girls – she'd turn their backs on the class and lift their frocks up and twamp them.

Anon

Rochdale Girls Gymnastic Display, c. 1905.

Spotland School photographed in 1905, but the same building which Jean remembers.

A Perfect School

Our teachers were two who were registered teachers and the rest were 'of good behaviour', church people, and I was brought up for my first few years with these teachers. They taught us reading, writing, arithmetic, sewing, history, everything – they were perfect!

We did a lot of mental arithmetic, and every child had to read in that day. Our teachers were friends. They used to come to my home, and I'd be in a Tuesday night and my mother would be ironing and my teacher would be mending socks. There was that atmosphere.

Margaret Turner

Spotland School

I didn't care for school. I can remember going as it was near where I am now, so I went across Spotland Road and in through the girls' entrance.

I struggled. English was my subject and in the top class this teacher used to read books and we would have to put the sentences into our own composition and I seemed to manage that alright. But I can remember two boys in that class: the poor things I don't know what they did or didn't do, but two or three times a week they had the cane out in front of us all. Well, Spotland School, I didn't think much of it.

Jean Roberts

Infants

We lived in New Moston then – a little community all of its own. It was like living in the country, with open fields. My brother was twenty months older than me and already started school. We used to walk past a farm and the farmer had a bull in the field with a chain and a log and we always used to run past covering anything red up like mad to get to school.

I was a little feared of it at first and the mistress seemed very severe. My particular pal said, 'She's alright and if she comes near I'll kick her.' That cheered me up no end! But I was a bit annoyed in one respect. Part of the infants must have started at a much younger age because every afternoon they put beds out and these little ones used to go to sleep. I used to think, 'Why can't I have a bed and go to sleep, we've got to work.'

Subjects, well we had art and handicraft, music and maths, but I can't remember that I was taught to read and write at school. My impression was that I had a knowledge of it; our parents taught us.

Ron Burrows

Derby Street School

I remember Derby Street. It was tall and dark with green paint. We had trays of sand. Drawing was my speciality or making models.

The second day after I'd been to school I went home, but my mother just said, 'Come on, I'll take you back'.

Alan Mills

Local Custom

I can remember the schoolteacher asking, 'What does your mother bake bread in?' and I said, 'A baking mug' and she said, 'Come out and stand in the front with your hands on your head.' So I stood there, I was in disgrace.

She asked other people and they all gave the same answer. Soon there was a whole row of us standing on the floor there. The headmistress came in and she said, 'Marjorie, what are you doing standing there?' I told her and she said, 'Come back to your place, all of you' and she tore a strip off the teacher, she said, 'This is what we do in Lancashire.'

Anon

Going by Bus to Secondary School

Then of course it was a change to Greenhill. A bus down to town and a walk up Toad Lane. Then coming home at night you walked down to town and maybe made a detour to be with others, and then got the bus home.

Kath Ward

Speech Day

Speech Day was in the chapel. You sat in rows with your legs the same way, all stockings to the same height. We had the morning to go down there and practise, then home in the afternoon to make sure your blouses were clean and your gym-slips pressed. The teachers sat us all in height order, so I was always at the back. The choir wore special ties.

Some chairman of the education committee at one of those speech days was introducing the choir and he said, 'The choir will now sing "When daisies peed"'.

Anon

Uniform

The gym-slips had box-pleats which sort of bulged, tied at the waist. When we went first there weren't summer dresses, they were introduced while we were there. They were plain green in a horrid sort of material, and the most peculiar sort of hats you could ever imagine. You had to put a pleat in them and they had a brim that turned up at the back and down at the front, and a badge on them 'Grace with Dignity'.

Barbara Eldred

Distinction

I sat the exam and passed to go to Greenhill, but for some reason my parents decided I should go to Fleece Street, which was a black gym-slip and a yellow sash, black and yellow tie. Now there I did like it a little bit better. Well I remember one thing – gymnastics. You lay on your back and had to put your legs right up in the air, holding your buttocks at the back so you went straight up. I was the straightest in the class so I stood out the wrong way round, didn't I? We had bookkeeping and we also had to go on Saturday morning for typing. Well, I got through the four years there okay and went into an accountant's office.

Jean Roberts

Free Books

There was a sort of initiation ceremony the first day, you know. They'd take you in the toilets and try to put your head down the

A class at Smithy Bridge School, with two of the girls wearing gymslips.

Class of 1925: a sixth form picnic at Millcroft Gardens.

School sports: members of the sixth form at the Girls' Secondary School, 1926.

toilet, that sort of thing – but it was over after a day or so.

North Manchester High School was a very prestigious place. My brother was already there and my parents were quite pleased because they didn't have to purchase the books. Usually what happened, the boys who were leaving put out tables and sold on their books to the boys who were coming up, but when it came to my age we didn't have to pay and all got brand-new books as well, issued by the education committee. My parents thought that was marvellous.

Ron Burrows

Drama

There was a Dramatic Society and I'd done a lot of activities at the church so when they asked for people I just put my name forward without thinking. They put on a play called *Emil and the Detectives*. I was Little Ginger – too little to play with the gang and had to sit at home and man the telephone while they were all out trying to capture the criminals.

There was a poetry-speaking competition. Anyway we won the thing and got to choose the prize, but it was a picture for the school. But the mistress was so pleased she gave us a packet of toffees each out of her own pocket. She was up on a pedestal in our eyes after that!

Ron Burrows

Getting Wet

We had swimming lessons and the person who was doing it, her mother was helping.

They had these long cords to put round someone who couldn't swim and the mother was doing me and I was hopeless. I got hold of this thing and pulled her in the bath. So I wasn't very looked upon, everyone was against me. She was this person's mother so she was getting on a bit to be pulled in.

Jean Roberts

Progress in Maths

I took the exam for the secondary school and my friends had taken it the year before and they all went to Central School. I didn't want to go to the secondary school and I can remember my father saying, 'I want you to go' and I went stomping all over the street to wear off my vexation.

I was in 3A and we had Miss Posnett for our teacher. She taught us English – I have very happy memories of Miss Posnett. Unfortunately I was always absent when they started algebra and geometry and I never did get the hang of it. I got a pass in maths and geography but it was essential to have a credit in maths to get matriculation – I could do trig' though!

Anon

Nicknames

I remember Mr Baraclough. He had a bald head and the boys called him Peanut. When you were asked to give some sort of dimension, he wouldn't accept measurements, you had to give comparisons. That was one – 'Is it as big as a peanut?'

He once asked me the height of a triangle on the blackboard and I hadn't the slightest idea – 'Your little pussy-cat could have done better than that' he said.

Ronnie Kershaw

A Convent Education

I went to a convent before we moved to Rochdale. In the very early days of going to school, it was country. I used to go past the blacksmith and he made an early start. He'd got the horse's rear leg up between his legs and something hot warming up the horse's shoes. I can particularly remember the smell. It fascinated me and I stood there for ages. Then further along there was the beginning of one of those parades of shops. There was a man called Mr Dinner and he used to repair shoes in his shop window and he had all these little tiny nails in his mouth and he used to slap the sole on and hammer it on and polish it. Well, I used to wait until he'd done both shoes, but I used to set off so very early!

I loved my time at the convent, it was such a loving atmosphere; the nuns were wonderful. We had Wednesday afternoon off and we went Saturday morning for peculiar things like deportment, music and dancing lessons. For deportment you'd walk around with a book on your head and learn how to sit and what to do with your legs. This was education you see, and quite different from anything I learnt at Rochdale. I sort of bluffed my way through there! My mother said, 'Should you be learning about laundry?' so I asked and the nun said, 'Oh, you won't need to do the laundry!'

Pamela Hutchinson

A 1939 High School production of Pride and Prejudice *with Pamela (second from the right) as* Mr Wickham .

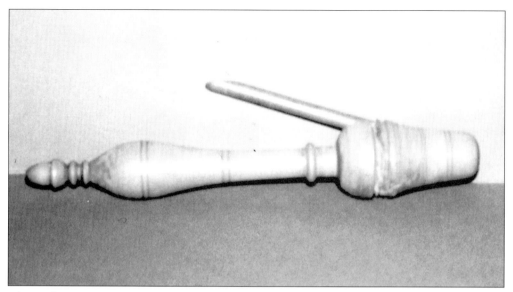

The teacher's clicker – it would gain the attention of six classes!

School in the 1910s

I went to a church school at Healey. The road you had to walk on went uphill, up along Whitworth Road which was a busy road but not busy compared to what it is now, and then you turned up a little lane across the fields.

I remember during the First World War the field we walked through was planted with what we used to call 'budgets' [swedes] and we used to pinch them and take them to school. We'd put them under our jerseys. You'd find a chap taking it, taking a great big bite, and putting it back. It was frowned on by the staff.

The school was built about 1850. It was really one big room divided by a partition. They still used the old standards: when you were thirteen you had to reach standard seven and then you could leave to go to work part-time. At fourteen you could go to work fully. The schoolteacher had started training at fourteen as a monitor and gradually worked his way up and finished as headmaster. He taught altogether about forty years in the same school and didn't retire until he was about seventy-five. We used to call him Joe Boss. He had a 'clicker'. When he was sitting at his desk in the middle of the school with six classes, about 240 people, he gave that little click because he wanted to make some kind of announcement.

I remember particularly object lessons. You had a rolled-up picture on the blackboard and these notes provided by the old school board and I remember one about foods and farming. It was on the morals of saving food by peeling potatoes thinly, and he said, 'I know you'll say it doesn't matter because if you have a pig the thick peel goes to the pig, but many people don't do that.'

Ronnie Kershaw

New premises at Balderstone for Rochdale High School for Boys. Brian Randale, craft teacher, with his form around 1960.

CHAPTER 4

Shoppers and Shopkeepers

Alan (centre) in front of the Pioneer Co-op on Pomona Street in 1931. Also pictured is the shop's manager Mr Wright (on the right).

Corner Shops

People in those days spent their time very differently. Shopping was an expedition. On Saturday everyone used to go into town and shop, going from shop to shop, supplying their needs for a week or so, but things changed when the war started.

All the streets had their corner shops and you had your favourite shops for various things, but people usually bought most of their weighty stuff in the street where they lived.

But you might have a particular fancy for Lipton's tea or Maypole butter or Brandon & Clegg's bacon and people used to go from shop to shop to buy these specialities.

Alan Mills

Yorkshire Street: Redman's, the Maypole Dairy and Woolworths.

From Door to Door

Competition between the shops was very keen. Duckworth's used to sell a milk-loaf, two pound in weight, for fourpence halfpenny, freshly baked at the bakery and very nice light bread. The old Duckworth used to go round from house to house with a grocery basket over his arm selling tea which he'd packed up. Eventually he was able to buy a shop and then about fifty shops. Their main shop was really chock-a-block. Everything was lovely and fresh though. You could smell the coffee half-way up Yorkshire Street.

Alan Mills

Fresh Coffee

The bigger grocers used to roast their own coffee, Duckworth's, Buckley's, and people would say, 'I'm going to such-and-such a grocer's because their coffee smells nice and fresh.' But some of the shops had a trick of going in the cellar with a little pile of ground coffee on a shovel and sticking it on a gas ring. The smell would come up through the grille in front of the shop – the tricks of the trade!

Alan Mills

'Coffin Nails'

Wholesalers used to supply all the shops, except the Co-op, they had their own warehouse. We sold candles and tapers because people had to use these to light the gas, bundles of firewood for kindling. There were sultanas and currants to pack up like a sleeve of fruit, and sugar – the paper bags weighed fairly heavy so I think they made a bit of profit. We sold tobacco loose. The boss always weighed that up! Woodbines we used to call 'coffin nails'. They were five for twopence in a packet.

Alan Mills

Choosing Your Bacon

When packed stuff started coming in, people said, 'Oh, I'm not paying for a packet' and we said, 'Packed stuff will never take off' and now of course everything's packeted, even the bacon.

At one time you used to go into the grocer's and it was always on the roll, and you'd have it cut according to the way you wanted it, thick or thin, and if you didn't like the look of it, you'd say, 'I'll have it from that other roll'. You might choose two or three rolls because one was leaner, but your husband liked it fatty so you'd have some fatty bacon.

Alan Mills

Spoilt for Choice

The biscuits were in containers with glass tops, tilted up so you could see. They'd ask, 'Do you want them mixed?'

Pamela Hutchinson

Weighing and Packing

Margarine seemed to start off in packets – Blue Band, Echo, Stork – but butter used to come in hundredweight barrels, and that had to be cut and wired through so you could get a piece of it. Lard was always loose, fifty-six pound

A carter on Yorkshire Street.

37

blocks. Even sugar had to be weighed out. It used to come in two-hundredweight sacks and it was packed in blue bags, two pound and three pound with the tops folded in.

Flour too; people must have baked a lot more than they do today. That shop used to take in a load of flour and we used to weigh it up into three and a half, seven and fourteen pound bags. The three and a half were the most popular, but even so it was a lot of flour to go every week. There could be about four or five of us on Monday weighing up the flour and it used to be terrible. I think that's what caused my catarrh. It used to take us all morning to weigh up this flour. The Co-op had an employee called the flour boy.

Alan Mills

Delivery

Sugar when it came always went upstairs. A lorry came and the back of the rear wheel had a spindle on it, and he'd put it into gear, the spindle would turn, and we used to get this gantry upstairs and drop the rope down. The lorry man would fasten on the bag, the spindle would turn and we'd swing the gantry. We used to have to hang out to get it but I never knew of anyone falling out. Potatoes went upstairs too and came down a chute into the basement while sugar was stacked up on the back benches and it took from Thursday till late on Friday to weigh the sugar up.

Alan Mills

Delivery vehicles on Cheetham Street, c. 1900. Plumbers Hornby & Holt (Alan's mother's relatives) are replacing a shop window.

Service

I worked at one shop where we drew £200 a week. We used to supply two estates and we did about two hundred orders a week and the shop trade, so I'd think on average the bill for the week's groceries was seven and six to ten shillings. You see you could get a quarter of tea for fourpence.

There were six of us working in that shop, and you must remember the assistant had to get everything for you – a pound of sugar, a bar of soap, a pound of tea, then he'd cut the bacon – and so it took time. Everything had to be weighed up because it came in bulk. Sometimes the assistant had to walk all round the shop because at busy times the shop was full of people waiting, half an hour to an hour, particularly on Friday night when they'd draw their pay.

Alan Mills

Tick

Some people used to buy on tick. They'd put it on a slate and pay so much a week. They usually paid quite regularly.

Alan Mills

Bad Payers

My uncle moved from south to north Manchester as his customers wouldn't pay their bills, 'You can't come to the front door, go round the back' they'd say. They were reluctant to pay.

Ron Burrows

Paying

In the bigger stores they had the compressed air. You'd put the cash into a little tube and you could hear it 'oooh' as it was sucked away, then it would come back out. In the old Provident Store in Lord Street they had a system of wires going like little tracks all round the store and a little carriage on them. The assistant used to put money in it and put it back on.

That's how it was at Turner's, I remember the sound it made: 'din-din'.

The Group

Carrying it Home

Most families had wicker baskets. They might take them to the grocer's and leave an order which would be packed for them when they were going home from work. If it didn't go in a basket, they'd make a little parcel with paper and string – now it's a plastic bag for everything. Butter was wrapped in grease-proof and bread in tissue-paper. Lots of families had carpet-bags (a couple of sheets of carpet sewn down with leather handles) and kids used to carry these while their mother probably had the basket. Then there were carrier-bags. They were quite useful till it rained and everything dropped out of the bottom of the bag.

Alan Mills

Delivered to Your Door

There used to be lots of deliveries, it was part of the service. The Co-op particularly did a lot of deliveries, with the name on the

Alan's Savoy Café, decorated for the Coronation in 1953.

side of the cart. Stuff could be picked up from the goods station.

Handcarts were used a lot too – the only way people could move heavy goods from one place to another, as there weren't any cars and they couldn't afford a horse. Plumbers in particular put all their pipes and tools on carts and pushed these through the streets.

The Group

Changes

After the war things changed. People were able to buy for a day or two instead of just from day to day: milk would keep longer, bacon, butter and cheese and some of the other perishable things.

Then people got washing-machines, and then there were televisions, so people had more time and they would think, 'I'm not going shopping, I'm going to watch telly this afternoon.' At this time the self-service stores came into being, and that made a difference to shopping because people found they could go to the store and get everything they wanted; then cars became popular.

So the small shops that had done all these good deeds for people in the past, people knew them and supported them personally from year to year and if they ordered something specially got it for them, that seemed to go by the board because convenience seemed to be taking over from people being kind in that way. Soon the small shopkeeper was feeling the pinch, they couldn't stock all the food and they used to say, 'Well, if we haven't got it we'll get it for you,' but people didn't want that any more, they wanted it there and then.

At one time, just to save twopence, people would say, 'I'm not going to buy that here', because in those days that twopence was a couple of bus fares, or a newspaper and what have you, and it made a big difference if you could just save that bit extra.

Alan Mills

Th'Oyle Man

King's Hardware had pans swinging from the ceiling. The authorities now would throw their hands up over the paraffin that was stored on the premises. You could take your own gallon can.

It used to be delivered by th'oyle man. He used to come round with a horse and cart, delivering paraffin and fire-lighters. They used to be four sticks of wood and wood shavings in the middle, bound around and wrapped in brown greasy paper. Even in the 1950s, a man used to come round with every type of hardware and soap. He even used to ring a bell.

The Group

Shrimp Stall

These barrow boys used to sell potted shrimps. Morecambe Bay was full of shrimps. They used little enamel cups to gather them up, and then you had them in a little pot with butter over the top. They had a salt-cellar and celery as well. You can see the site marked out where they had the original Rochdale market.

Alan Mills

Black Peas

Then there were black peas, they came round in a boiler. The man had a little barrow with a fire in and you took your own basin.

There was a big black dog lived near me who adored these black peas. Every time he used to come, the man would put a few on the pavement for this dog.

Once the lads played a trick on him. He'd graduated from the barrow to a little horse and trap. He used to be fond of drinking and half-way round he'd stop at the pub. They unharnessed his horse, put the shafts of his cart through the gate and put the horse in on the other side so he couldn't find it!

Barbara Eldred, Ronnie Kershaw

A Tasty Snack

There used to be a stall at the bottom where Lloyds Bank is now, and there was an old woman there selling these black puddings. When I used to go to night-school – not every week but when I could afford it – I used to come out and buy one of these for twopence. She'd slice it and put some mustard on and wrap it in a piece of paper and I'd eat it going down the Church Steps.

Alan Mills

Above and below: *End of terrace advertisements on Bolton Road.*

CHAPTER 5

Hard Work

Joan's mother, standing on the left wearing a hat, at the mill's Christmas footing in the late 1930s.

Health and Safety

My grandfather used to make balata belting – they used it on these big flywheels as drive-belts for machines – and they must have used benzene in the production of it in some way. I was only little, but I remember he always used to come home reeking of it. He lived till he was ninety.

I used to work in Turner's offices, at the top where Sir Samuel Turner had his office. I used to go and clean his cupboard when I first started work. I remember Miss Cudworth who was his secretary saying, 'Do be careful when you're taking things out.' I got these big rocky things out and it was raw asbestos, a sort of bluey green, lovely and silky.

Barbara Eldred

Asbestos

They used to have a little train coming down the hillside and that had the raw asbestos. The railway went to the top, then

Mills: Kelsall and Kemp's (demolished in 1962).

it was taken down to the works in these little trucks.

They used it on shipping as insulation round the boilers. It was puddled and stuck on like a kind of clay.

We used it at the café too, to light the boiler.

In beer there's a little bit at the bottom that's cloudy and to clear it they used a sort of bucket with this asbestos called theorit, a type of wadding. They'd pour the beer through this and it used to come out sparkling clear, all the residue left in the asbestos. The factory who made that was in Ashton, but then they closed down because it was unsafe for people to work in.

They say it was the wives died of asbestos poison because they washed the men's clothes.

The Group

The 'Knocker-up'

My mother came from Bolton when she got married. After she'd had me she had to get a job obviously, so she went to work at a mill just up the street from where we lived, called the Grove Mill, and she was a weaver, a good one. I can remember waking up in the morning with the 'knocker-up' coming, and on the top of his pole was all the bones out of corsets – you know in those days we had very strong corsets on. The wires that was in were all curled round and plaited and very flexible with a brass safety cover on each end. The knocker-up used to have this huge pole that would reach the bedroom window and he used to have about half a dozen of these metal things on his pole. When he came it would be about five o'clock in the morning and it would be like this 'rat-tat-

tat' on the window, and my dad had to jump out of bed and knock on the window to say he'd got up. He knocked everybody up for so much a week – it wasn't very much from each house. Then my mum got up and you could hear all the workers going to the top of the street. You could hear all these clogs clattering up the street, but my mum never, ever wore clogs. She thought she was a little bit above that sort of thing.

Joan Thomson

Child Care

Everybody round where we lived, they all worked in the mill, so it made it that the lady next door at that time was called Mrs Schofield and she was present when I was born. She was one of those women who wore a black dress down to her ankles and a white pinny and she was very, very strait-laced. I nicknamed her Scoddy and she used to come and do to me and then when I started school it made it a little bit easier, did that, except for school holidays. So as I was getting older I had to go to an old hand at New Hey and stay there for the school holidays.

In those days the teachers only had about two weeks, not six like they do now. When my mother went to work at Pilling's there was a man that used to work near her and they called him Little Joe because his knees were together like that and he was nearly on the floor. In those days they couldn't do anything for him. So it was a case of 'You go and stop with Uncle Joe,' and she used to give him coppers because he'd had to pack up because of his legs. They used to look after me and give me my tea.

Joan Thomson

Half-Timers

By the time I was twelve we had done all we could at St Alban's Day School. Five of us got these scholarships, so we worked with these other teachers to look after the small ones, just to relieve the teachers. Another friend said to me, 'Oh, we're poor' so I said, 'So are we' and she said, 'I'm going for a job'. I said, 'Well, I'll go with you', so we both went off to the Union Mill and got a job as half-time doffers. Half a crown, half a day, they started six in the morning till half past twelve, and half past one till half past five. We went and worked in the afternoon for the first time and when I came out I was all cottony. When I got home, my mother said, 'You're very late, where have you been?' and it was a day before I could tell her where I'd been. She was very annoyed and said, 'You've made your bed, you lie on it.' I was twelve and a half. You could leave school at thirteen, so my mother made me stick it.

Margaret Turner

On Your Bike

My first job was in the office, in a garage. The man there was very sarcastic. No one left, they were usually sacked, but I didn't think there was much opportunity, so I went to telephones then. In the meantime, I'd been for an interview as a telephonist at Birch Hill Hospital, and they asked me at the interview if I could ride a bicycle! I suspect some of the duties finished at ten o'clock, and you'd have to get home some way or other. I started going to night-school after that, and I've been going to night-school and college ever since.

Anon

Ronnie's father maintained the tram wires.

The First Job

When it came to school leaving time, there was a job going in the town hall, and my father being in office work said, 'You'd better go and get it'. At the interview there were a number of lads there and a fellow called Butterworth got the job. He'd been working at John Bright's, so when I got home my father said, 'Why don't you go and get his job?' So I went in and said I was enquiring after the vacancy in the carpet department.

The manager, Wroth, hadn't realized there was a vacancy, but they needed someone with particularly good handwriting for addressing labels. Then there was a vacancy in the Co-op and I stayed there nearly ten years. I liked working with my hands. I went to grocery classes in the old college for three or four years to get my Institute of Grocers certificate and meanwhile I went to the College of Art in the evenings for writing posters.

Alan Mills

Coal Miners

They used to mine coal around the Cheeseden Valley. During the miners' strikes, a lot of people opened up the mines. I remember my father and his pals going. You know where John Bright's is, on Whitworth Road, at the back of that there are mines driven into the hillside, the area's riddled with mines. They went into the mine to the far end and in those days they didn't use pit-props, they left pillars of coal to hold the roof up. They went into the mines, took the pillars out, came back and the roof fell in behind them. But it kept a supply of coal going – we were never without coal.

Ronnie Kershaw

Water for Steam Trains

There used to be a little mine down Smithy Bridge Road, going to the station and they used to have a pumping station on there. You could hear it 'pump-pump-pump-pump' night and day as the water was pumped out. At that time on the railway they had those troughs so when the trains ran through they could collect their own water. This mine kept those troughs full of water.

The Group

Brickworks

There were far more people coming into the town, so many more houses and mills and chimneys were being built. There were New Hey bricks – a very hard brick more like Accrington, and Bentley Street brickworks.

Railway bridge at Wardleworth with the shields for the Lancashire and Yorkshire railways.

Their bricks used a bluey clay, high fired and slightly smaller. They gave up about thirty years ago when they ran short of clay. They went as far back as they could – it was quite a cliff with two houses on top.

Alan Mills, Ronnie Kershaw

Union Action

While my mother was working at the Grove they decided they would start this trade union business. It was a Mr Ernest Thornton, he was just up-and-coming in those days and he came to the Grove this particular day and he told everyone in the mill he wanted everybody out and they were

47

going to strike for more money. So my mother, she said no, she wasn't doing that. She came home and said, 'I can't afford to strike for more money, I've got to be content with what I've got.' So anyway she was blacklegged for this and I know she went to work this particular day and had to go through all this barrage of people. It was horrendous. A few more were working beside her and they came back to our house and I had to go in the cellar out of the way. They were threatening to smash in the windows and all this, just because she was too proud to tell them that she couldn't afford to strike. We wouldn't have had anything to eat if she'd gone out on strike – some of the other women, their husbands perhaps had more reasonable jobs.

I think it was towards winter-time and in those days my dad didn't have any work to do in winter because nobody wanted their houses decorated – they'd no central heating, only coal fires, and they didn't want it making damp. So my dad's total amount of money used to be the dole if he could get it. If not, he used to go round on his bike with a bucket of whitewash asking people did they want the cellars and the toilet whitewashing to get a few coppers in – just coppers, you wouldn't believe it, would you.

Joan Thomson

Long Hours, Low Pay

In the shop we worked from seven till seven, and eight in the morning till four on Saturdays, while the shops in town used to stay open till eight or nine on Saturdays. We did have Tuesday afternoons, but no extra days – we were always a bit aggrieved when Christmas came on a Saturday!

There was a lot of unemployment in the early 1930s. We actually had a reduction in wage because of the reduction in living costs, so we were getting too much money. My wage was dropped by half a crown. It just shows how tight money was in those days. There was a confectioner near us and they used to make plate fruit tarts for threepence halfpenny. Sometimes three of us would share a fruit tart; we'd toss up for who paid the halfpenny!

Alan Mills

A Heading

The way a weaver's wage depended in those days – they used to put the beam in and the warp would be marked with blue at different intervals as it had been rolled onto the beam, and they had to work really hard to get that mark to come up so they could do what they called a 'heading'. They put the heading in and a red strand used to go before the blue mark and come after it so when it had gone round the roller at the front they could cut through it. She always got these cut-offs.

Joan Thomson

Blanket Sewing

I went blanket sewing. There used to be mills in Rochdale which put the piece on the blankets after they'd been woven. They were sent to Higham's Mill which is down in Sudden to be 'whipped' – we called it sewing. From there I went to the Dunlop Mill.

Margaret Turner

A fire at Dunlop Mill (but Margaret had a new career before then).

Tin

There was the tinsmith's. He made wash boilers and lading-cans. He used to have a little shop and a tinsmith's business at the back, and he used to make these lading-cans and hang them up all over the pavement, at the corner where the Pavilion was.

It was interesting on children's toys before the war. A lot of the stuff came from Japan and it was the off-cuts from making tin trays, tin where they'd put a lithograph label on it. They were sold to these toy manufacturers, so often the bottom of your toys would have a little design on referring to something completely different.

Alan Mills, Ron Burrows

Cheeses and Mops

Samuel O'Neill's paper tubes at Castleton – I remember the smell it used to make.

They made cones for cotton, called 'cheeses', reds and blues, probably covered in some sort of lacquer.

Then Becket's came in and started making foil for cigarettes and that sort of thing, and of course they used copper – they're clearing it up now.

Goodhew's made some sort of chemical for putting into the boiler and taking all the scale off.

Besco made mop heads, Casson's did bottling at the Roche Brewery. There was Heap's Dyeworks, Eagle Oil.

The Group

The River Spodden at Foot Mill. Turner Bros works lie to the left of the picture.

The River Spodden at Spotland Bridge, c. 1910. The road leads on to Foot Mill and Turner Bros.

Jobs for Lads

There were lots of little foundries that cast wheels for people building machines for the factories – Jane Street, Silver Street, Ashworth Street.

Just at the end of Champness Hall Buildings there's a metal archway that used to say 'Mason's Foundry'. If you go up by Iveson's wall of huge stone blocks, that was the side of the foundry where they made castings for Petrie McNaught's when they were starting off as engine builders. Holroyd's did a lot of bronze castings, and Holt's on Whitehall Street had a big foundry casting for their own machinery.

Then there were pattern makers, that was a highly skilled trade, and moulders. All the lads wanted to get an apprenticeship at Robinson's. They made woodworking and flour-milling machinery; they built plants all over Russia, Australia, America, a huge organization. And Turner's – everyone worked at Turner's at some time in their life.

The Group

Buckley Mill as Jim saw it, dressed for the Coronation in 1937.

Getting Started

My father worked at Buckley Mill. Maintenance was carried out at holiday times, so I ended up hanging around on the off chance of watching some job being done. Always at the annual holidays the boiler was 'blown down' and all the flues cleaned out, the boiler descaled and inspected and tested by the insurance company and any repairs carried out. I would wheedle my way in and be sent to get cigarettes and drinks (it was summer and thirsts needed quenching).

Occasionally I got to have a ride on the works' lorry, a three-ton Morris Commercial, painted green and immaculately kept by its driver, a Mr Swain.

My thirteenth birthday came in 1939, when school was taken over as a decontamination centre. I couldn't leave till I was fourteen and struggled on, looking for work. This operation consisted of obtaining a green card from the labour exchange and going to see firms where apprentices might be taken on.

Jim Barham

'Success to Buckley Mill': the mill in 1937.

Training as a Nurse

I wanted from the age of seven to be a nurse. I'd been in hospital with scarlet and diphtheria, and the under matron there used to come to our house for tea on her half day because she and my mother did handwork. She became my best auntie, I called her Auntie Shoo. I lived in Barclyde Street in a four-bedroom house. The rent was two and threepence per week and my mother did sewing for people.

Near there was a gentlemen's club. This lady that was stewardess had no children and she used to sit and talk to me when I was a little girl. After I had the scarlet fever she said to my mother, 'Why don't you let your little girl come and play in the grounds' and I used to go shopping with her and my brother used to go to the pictures with her husband: we became family friends. When I was sixteen I went up at night and I used to wash the glasses just to help and I started helping them to serve one or two drinks. Managers and people used to bring me chocolates and little gifts but I'd never been paid, so the committee decided to pay me two pounds a month. That I was allowed to keep, but I didn't have money when I was twenty like they have today. I used to work in the mill during the day and then work at night to get some money because I wanted to go nursing.

My mother clung to me. We were very good friends, only the two of us. I was thirty and there was a boy who was very friendly but he was a Catholic and I was Protestant and in those days it wasn't done. So my mother said, 'Do you still want to go nursing?' so I said 'Yes', so she said, 'Well, you can.' I was thirty! I'd never been away from home I'd had such care, and I went to London.

Margaret Turner

A Nursing Career

With being older, I got an awful lot of responsibility; the matron was from Bury, and the next one was from Preston. I was the only Lancashire girl. There were no drugs in those days – you nursed the patient. I had the first oxygen tent that came into England. There was a little girl and she was black when she came in so she was put in this oxygen tent. They're cased in but you can put your hand in and attend to their needs, and in an hour that little face became pinker and pinker. Oh, if you saw nursing as we did – with care, with love, and you had to know all about them, and you saw those little things come to life – oh, it paid.

Matron sent for me just before Christmas and said, 'We're going to send you on a midwifery course so we're going to send you home first for a week's holiday.' When I came home my mother was surprised: 'Oh,' she said, 'you can't do midwifery, you've never seen a baby born, you don't know anything about it. When you see a baby being born, think of a rose coming through, the petals just opening and the beautiful face coming through.'

I'd been there two years as theatre nurse when Matron sent for me. 'You've got to go home,' she said 'your mother's not well.' So I came home, that would be 1939-1940. I came here and had to do some work so I got a school nurse's post at Bury. Then I was friends with the coroner at Rochdale. I'd known him since I was a little girl, he was only born round the corner from me and he was sixteen years older. So I got married and looked after my mother, and they both died within a year of each other.

Margaret Turner

Christmas in the mill works canteen in the 1950s.

Shut Down

Unfortunately the mill closed down and my mother had to go to the dole and they wouldn't give her any money because they found her a job at Red Lumb at Norden, the only available place. It meant setting off in the morning about five o'clock and she didn't get home until seven. She must have been absolutely exhausted because they worked Monday to Saturday, and Saturday until half past twelve. So she'd only Saturday and Sunday to catch up on her washing and ironing – washing was in a dolly-tub with a rubbing board, which my dad used to help her with. Then she managed to get a job at a mill called Pilling's, at the opposite side of the street from the Grove. Then funnily enough, that closed.

Joan Thomson

The Boss

When Pilling's was packing up, she managed to get to get a job at Mitchell Hey Mill on Bury Road and Mellor Street. It was quite a big mill, and this was a man called Mr Francis Shackleton that owned it and he came from Hebden Bridge. A typical mill owner, a big man he was, bushy eyebrows, bushy white hair. By this time it was going up to the war years and she was weaving moleskin and Bedford cord for trousers, and she'd a duck and an ordinary calico. In the winter the boss used to walk down. She had a run-in with him first of all because he comes walking down the alley with his hands in his pocket, jingling his keys and what have you, and everyone goes like this to him. My mother just stood there and just smiled. So when he were ready to walk on he come back and spoke

Getting home: waiting for the Wardle bus on Smith Street in the 1940s.

in her ear, 'Why dost tha not touch thee forelock t'me?' and she said, 'My work is good enough for that to warrant me a job so I don't need to touch my forelock to anyone.'

Well, the next run-in she had with him – she came down this particular day and it was bitter cold and they were working with their coats on and gloves with the fingers cut out. So she went up to him as he was walking down. 'Mr Shackleton, is it possible to have some steam put through the pipes?' – there was pipes all over up above – and he just looked at her and says, 'Why?' She says, 'Because we're all so cold' so he comes to her ear and says, 'If tha's feeling cold, get all the looms working and come up to me and I'll give thee a skipping-rope and tha can skip in the alley, that'll keep thee warm.'

Joan Thomson

Tea-Break

Apart from that they had some good times in the mill. They had a big boiler in the cellar where all the cops were kept in tins and different types of material. My mother was one of them, she was always there for seven o'clock (they started at half past) and filled four cans up with these cops so that she didn't need to go in the cellar till dinner-time. As soon as they stopped the mill she'd go straight in, fill all her cans up before she had her dinner. She never left her alley.

They had a brew mid-morning and one at dinner-time, consisting of a spoonful of tea, a spoonful of sugar and a spoonful of condensed milk, this was run onto newspaper and this was pulled over and the ends folded in. When you wanted a brew you used to take your pot, put all this into the pot, stir it up and let it settle and that used to be your cup of tea.

Joan Thomson

No Sitting Down

I left school at fourteen. My first job was at a confectioner's not far from where we lived. I had to start at six in the morning till six at night. I hadn't to sit down – there was nowhere to sit. I was scrubbing tins out and things like that all day because this shop was very, very busy. They used to cook their own ham and pork and all like that. It was really nice stuff they had. I could eat anything that there was, but I had to stand up to do it and for that I got seven and six a week.

Joan Thomson

The Apprentice

My working apprenticeship came at last, at W. Hurst's. With some trepidation I put on my overalls, mounted my bike and rode off for my first big day.

My first tasks were to open the two padlocked gates. Back inside the works, I was put under Mr J. Bracken's wing. Mr Joe was a remarkable man. He came to work dressed in a suit, shirt, collar and tie and wore a cap. He then changed into a special waistcoat which held a 0.1 micrometer, small set square, six inch rule and other equipment. He would tell me what was needed for a particular job and I would pack them into a Gladstone bag, then we would walk or take the bus to various jobs.

As the year wore on, I made a pilgrimage to my 'Mecca', the Eclipse Mill, to deliver a part. The engineer asked if I wanted to look around. With instructions to keep on the calico, he took me to gaze in awe at the gleaming piston-rods and crankshaft rocking to and fro with such majestic power, driving the ropes which reached twenty, thirty, a hundred feet up to each floor to drive carding machines, mules and cotton-breaking machines. Afterwards I would plod reluctantly to my own small workshop.

Jim Barham

No Job Too Big or Too Small

Whenever the bell rang I had to see who was calling. Once it was a little old lady with a copper kettle that needed a patch putting over a small hole. Another day I answered the bell and a lady stood there with a box about three feet six inches long. We took the box into the workshop to find an artificial leg inside! The ankle pin had moved out of alignment. It was two to three hours' work to fix and they didn't charge her anything. Then there was the Crossley gas engine, converted to diesel, at Harry Travis's cotton waste mill. This became overloaded occasionally and would do its big end bearing in.

Red cabbage cutting machines came in about once a year. These were a large chute into which a red cabbage was fed to be pushed up against a rotating disc into which four cutters were fixed. We would clean and paint the metalwork and sharpen and reset the cutters. The pickle works had a hand-operated jar-capping machine which we serviced too.

We also serviced a good lot of rubber machinery – a dirty, heavy and often very hot job as the rubber was made out of sulphur, carbon black and various additives mixed in a rolling-mill and put into moulds in a hydraulic press.

As time went on we made machines for the dyeing trade, cross ball winding machines, and timing chain wheels for tanks until I was called up for the Army.

Jim Barham

Learning to Weave

There was three options when you went on the dole in those days – munitions, the forces or the cotton, because they needed the cotton, you see. I couldn't pass any medicals for the forces or munitions – it was very strict for munitions and I used to get a lot of bronchitis, so it had to be cotton. So I was learning with my mother. Well, she was a tyrant, she was really. It didn't stop when we went home from work because she'd start on me, 'It's like dragging an iron horse, trying to teach her something' and I was only doing like the rest of the young ones that were in. There were about twelve of us (aged fourteen) all learning to be weavers.

Finally I got my own set of looms which were back beams to my mother's. If I wanted the toilet, it was 'oo-oo, oo-oo' like this, and she'd look up, 'Don't let it take you five minutes' she'd say. A lot of the girls my age, they'd be stood in the toilet smoking. I had a moleskin, a duck and two calicoes. Both the moleskin and the duck, you'd never, ever to let an end break. If it did, you'd to stop the loom immediately and pull it all back, which entailed a lot of hard work. You'd got to wind the loom back and you'd got to scratch it all out until you'd got it back to where you'd started from. You know how young people are if you're not just watching every second! The next thing you get what they called a track, where the loom had banged the shuttle up and you'd get all the ends out for about so far and it would just carry on weaving, you see. Whenever I saw anything like that – oh dear me, it used to make me feel sick because I knew my mother would be coming into the alley. She'd give me such a crack over the ears. But she had to make sure all her cuts came off at these blue marks as they should and she'd get thirty shillings a week, and that is keeping at it every second. If I had to go for more cops she'd keep my looms going as well. If she saw one stopping she'd run in and start it off again.

Joan Thomson

From Driving to Racing

My father was getting towards retirement at Buckley Mill, and the boss there, John Hanson, lived at St Anne's, where we'd always gone on holiday. The chauffeur they'd taken on never got there on time: he was always about an hour out, either way! So they sacked him and I applied for the job. First week I was on eight pounds ten a week – riches, you know – so I started on this new career.

There were three mills, then by the 1950s the Canadian job dried up a bit and the South African job fizzled out altogether, so it left them nothing much to do and it went bust. So then I was coming along New Road by Ratcliffe's Garage and Harry was working on a car outside. I knew him because we used to get petrol off him for all the cars for Buckley Mill,

Bales packed for export from Buckley Mill to South Africa or Canada in the late 1950s.

Moving machines at Buckley Mill, c. 1955.

and I said, 'What are you doing?' and he showed me and I said, 'Don't do it like that' and so I helped him. Then we built this racing car, and one or two more and I was the engineering side – modifying cylinder heads, filing things and all sorts – hands-on things.

We decided we'd start up a firm. We finished up with a Morris Minor with nearly everything there was in the saloon car racing job, all modified. Harry designed this fuel injection system, but we only ever got it to work once. We used to go down through Littleborough and to the top of Blackstone Edge and then down to the reservoir. That was our testing circuit and we got this Morris 1000 doing a 120 miles an hour past the New Inn, and then we developed it.

Jim Barham

Lifting gear at Buckley Mill in the 1950s.

Nursing After the War

In 1950 I was asked if I would start a new clinic. I lived in Cleveley's Avenue, off Oldham Road, above Balderstone church. So I went to Boundary Park and did VD work for five years. The places I had to go into, I just thought, 'If your mother and Stanley knew the places you went into!' I was allowed freedom in my job. I worked in the clinic some time. Sunday afternoon I went to Manchester after one or two men and they would be at the same address, Angel, near the docks where all these men from the ships lodged. I was only a little thing and I went in this place and said what I wanted, you were never allowed to use a name. I went in and it was very dark with rooms all round and great big men came out. I couldn't let anyone see me go to anyone else so I had to go out and come in again and found another man the same. I never had any trouble with any of them.

I had the pleasure of seeing Dr Steptoe start his work. Later I went back to Rochdale and worked until I retired in 1962.

Margaret Turner

Modernization

After the war I went back to do my four year stint. All the same bods were there doing all the same things, but they'd modernized a bit here and there, got a few new machines. It was all gas. In the morning you lit the Bunsen burner – a tube like that with a burner – it took five

Modernization? Taking up tram lines on Spotland Road.

minutes to heat up, then you switched the gas on. You had to start it by hand – three of us had to turn the engine and eventually it fired. I'd been back there a couple of months and this engine – it must have been put in about 1890 – the back end where it fired was corroded and it blew the end of the cylinder out, 'Vwoom!' Finished, scrapped, and not a bit of electricity in the place. Then we had to get a motor, run a cable down the main road, and so I finished up in the engineering bit.

Jim Barham

In the Laundry

After the war my husband got a job in Bristol and said he wasn't coming back any more, he was leaving me so I had to get a job. My mother said she'd look after the little boy so I went down to the Co-op laundry.

They'd advertised and with people coming back from the war there wasn't a right lot going. I was given a job on the calender. It's a huge machine, and if you have bedding or table-cloths, anything like that, it comes through all these rollers and when it comes out the other end it's completely ironed, immaculately ironed. So you're taking it off the rollers and it's boiling hot stuff – really hot – and you've got another woman at the opposite end to fold it with you.

Well, I was working with ever such a nice young woman. She was in lodgings, living with a man and she was pregnant. She used to come back at dinner-time and say, 'Oh, I have enjoyed my dinner' and I'd say, 'Have you, why what have you had?' and she said, 'I've had some lovely bread and butter and some pickled beetroot on it' and I used to think, 'My goodness me!' We were working there this particular day and I saw her go like this – flick something off – and I asked what she was doing. 'Oh, it's a tick,' she said, 'we all have them on us in the lodging house.' I couldn't wait for going home time.

Joan Thomson

The Best Weaver

I went down to Mitchell Hey and asked could I see Mr Shackleton. He said, 'What dost tha want to work for, I thought tha'd got married, with a little boy.' So I explained and he said, 'I can find thee a job, can ta start in t'morn? Weaving's too heavy for thee now, I know tha's not been so well, tha can come up in the warehouse.' That is where they put all the cuts on the table, they go through all the lot, pulling all the bits and pieces off and making it look perfect.

One day Mr Shackleton, he must have been very old by then, said to me, 'Any cuts that come up with those four numbers on, nobody in our warehouse ever needed to look at them. Tha mother's cloth were perfect – the best weaver I ever had!'

Joan Thomson

Above and below: *men and horses of Rochdale Corporation's Cleansing Department, c. 1910.*

CHAPTER 6

Time Out

The Regal Cinema ready for its grand opening by the Mayor of Rochdale on 16 May 1938.

The Cinema

There were eleven cinemas in Rochdale. The Palace was called the Palace Tudor, it was black and white you see on the outside. The Coliseum on Oldham Road was one of the oldest – it was called the flea-pit and was like a Nissen hut. Then there was the Ceylon, and up Trafalgar Street on the garage site was the Empire and the Hippodrome. The Victory was by the station and built just after the First World War. King's was at the corner of King's Road and Oldham Road – that's a bingo place now. The Regal (later the ABC and the Cannon) was the best – it had an organ and lovely decoration.

There were two in Castleton, the Ideal and the Princess, opposite one another. Oh yes, there was plenty of business, there were queues on Saturday night. They changed some pictures half-way through the week, and during the war you had to book. The machine used to break down, sometimes twice during one film!

The cinemas I went to just before the war, they used to come round in the interval, spraying perfume.

We used to sit on the back row, on the double seats!

The Group

Film Shows

They used to have these film shows at Union Street Chapel on Saturday nights. They were the only pictures you were allowed to go to on your own, they were inclined to be a religious type of picture like *Ben Hur*, or *The Ten Commandments*. Again there was competition for the back row! The ushers were always men from the chapel and kept an eye on the behaviour.

They took it down last year and there's a car park there now.

Jean Roberts

'A' Films

Young children used to stand outside if it was an 'A' film, and they used to say, 'Will you take us in missus?'

Anon

The Rialto

The Rialto used to have a little balcony. The projectionists used to get very hot, so they could go out and cool themselves down a bit.

The end of the Rialto – demolished in 1981.

Underneath was the café, then a glass verandah and at the end was an exit door, but everyone had to go out by the main door. They went to a great deal of trouble to make it really modern and anyone going would be able to see without sitting behind pillars. They had a firm called Booth's from Bolton and it was the biggest girder they'd built to that day and it supported the whole of the circle without any cross supports. The manager was a very big fellow and he said, 'When I go to the theatre the seats are always too small so I want bigger seats.' The front row in the circle, they were all larger seats than anywhere else. They had four director's boxes alongside the projection and they had basket chairs in. When I was courting we used to get free tickets and go in these boxes, even when the cinema was full, providing there was nobody in them!

Gracie Fields opened the Rialto in 1927 – it must have been a bit of a quiet evening, she just came and did it and that was it.

The seats were ninepence, one shilling, and one and six. When they first built it they were talking about whether they should

The Curtain Theatre

"MRS. MOONLIGHT"

March 29th—April 6th, 1941

Saturday Matinées: Doors open 2 10 p.m.
Commence 2 30 p.m.

Saturday Evenings: Doors open 6 10 p.m.
Commence 6 30 p.m.

Sunday Matinées: Doors open 2 10 p.m.
Commence 2 30 p.m.

Tuesday Evening: Doors open 6 25 p.m.
Commence 6 45 p.m.

A Curtain Theatre programme from 1941.

Programmes

The first film I saw was *Desert Song*. There was *Modern Times*, Harold Lloyd, *The Great Dictator* and then shows with dancing girls – *The Ziegfeld Follies*, Astaire and Rogers, Janette Macdonald and Webster Booth at the Empire. That was always popular and packed out.

The Pavilion had the better pictures. The Palace was very well established. The Victory, they were the first people to put the talkies in. Now there's not a single cinema left in Rochdale, not in the town.

The Group

have a stage behind – it was going to cost so much – two and a half thousand more to build a stage. They said it was too near Manchester to put decent shows on to warrant the expense. The end of the building was left a bit rough so they could add onto it if necessary and it actually cost £27,000 to put it up. They had an Italian to install marble steps and a special artist came and painted the Rialto Bridge in Venice on one of the panels over the stage, while the panels either side were painted with roses.

There was a veranda outside where you could wait if you had to queue in the rain.

Alan Mills, Barbara Eldred

Rochdale Alumni Dramatic Society

presents

Tomorrow's Child

(A Comedy in Three Acts) by

J O H N   C O A T E S

At

The Municipal High School for Girls Greenhill

on

THURSDAY 11th NOVEMBER
FRIDAY 12th NOVEMBER
SATURDAY 13th NOVEMBER
1948

PROGRAMME . . TWOPENCE

Programme for Rochdale Alumni Dramatic Society's 1948 production of Tomorrow's Child.

Drake Street – spot the difference!

Going Dancing

It was our way, was that, to go to these dances then. You danced with a partner – you could dance with your girlfriend, or with a boy if he asked you.

You had to learn to dance. We learnt by going to All Saint's dances, Miss Ogden on Drake Street, Rafferty on Yorkshire Street, or Turner's used to have regular dances with a four or five piece band and supper provided – there were quite a few. Midweek you'd have an hour of lessons then just dancing, then Saturday night was all dances. There were lots of semi-pro bands – it wasn't blaring music, but piano, violin.

They also had these girls, dance hostesses, you could pay sixpence to have a dance with, so you'd always have a partner even if you went on your own.

I never went to classes – just Sunday school, and picked it up at the dances there.

The Group

Dance Halls

The Carlton was just across from the Palace (the Universal Laundry took it over) started by four businessmen, Harold Firth and his friends. It was a lovely hall with a stage and a balcony all round and a restaurant as you went in. Saturday night you could go up in the balcony and watch the dancing for sixpence, 'Oh, there's so-and-so, who's she with?' There was a special sprung floor. Freddy Mark and his band were there for years before they went to Blackpool.

Electric House, illuminated in 1937.

There was the Masonic Hall and the Provident Hall in Lord Street, and the town hall, the Flying Horse, the Tudor Café and Sunday schools all had dances. People wore frocks, a dinner-jacket, you would dress up in a nice skirt and silk blouse or a suit; it got very casual later on.

The Group

Radio

You were never short of anywhere to go to be entertained, I mean you had no television of course, you had a radio, you went out and found your own interest and your own entertainment.

We made a crystal set, a gold type with brass wire. There was a flat battery and earphones, and you fiddled around with the 'cat's whisker' to make contact. There was a little shop where you could buy all the parts. Father then built a one-valve set with a big knob to turn and half a dozen terminals in a row. It stood on the fireplace for all of us to plug into.

Ron Burrows, Alan Mills

Safe at Night

It was safe going out then and we walked virtually everywhere. The buses used to finish at nine o'clock. During the war you walked in the blackout.

Jean Roberts, Sheila Jones

Traffic Problems

Traffic, well there were horse-drawn vehicles. People used to have very good back gardens because they were never short of the manure. The horses used to come regularly and you'd be going out with the shovel – people quarrelled over it!

Where I lived, people used to hang their clothes in the street and when a horse and cart came it was calamitous – there was all this washing!

Alan Mills, Anon

Family Walks

Nearly every Sunday evening, some aunts, uncles and cousins would come and if it was fine we'd go walking, up to the Donkey at Syke.

Sheila Jones

Cuckoo Flowers and Marsh Marigolds

The walk I remember is now the Hurst Estate, beside the cemetery. It was all fields then and we used to go up the lanes along there. But we used to go up Spotland Road first before we got there, it used to be a bit marshy and we'd see the cuckoo flowers and at Red Brook you could still see all the marsh marigolds. The cricket club's there now.

There was Hopwood, Healey Dell, lots of footpaths between farms.

Jean Roberts

Traffic calming? Maypole roundabout in 1937.

Healey Dell, a scene of early industry and later promenades.

Kath, in the middle of this family group, on an outing to Hollingworth Lake in August 1934.

Arrow Chases

We used to walk miles over Lobden and the Heys Hills. A group of lads would run and chalk arrows on the walls for an 'arrow chase'. Two would set off and we'd give them five minutes and we'd catch them in the end.

Ronnie Kershaw

Excursion by Bus

My father used to be an enthusiast for Hardcastle Crags. All the Rochdale buses, the double-deckers, had seats both sides but when you got on the Todmorden buses there used to be one big wide one right across and a passageway down the edge. Then the tickets were about that long, and they used to chop a little bit out in the middle. Ours were little short tickets with a round hole in.

Oh, it was fascinating going to Hardcastle Crags – a full day out and take a picnic. There's a hut where you used to get the hot water for your tea.

Jim Barham

Hollingworth Lake

People would go by train to Smithy Bridge station, then you could go on a steamer, across to the old rowing club pavilion. Sometimes the lake froze solid in the winter.

There was dancing outdoors on the wooden stage at Lake Side, by the Beach Hotel. The fair came at Easter and Whit, but there weren't as many entertainments as there used to be, when they called it the 'weavers' seaport'.

I remember the bobby horses – wooden horses about six feet high – with manes and tails. You could ride on them, they went by

71

gas. In the old days they were part of a steam ride; then they were sold off to America.

The Group

A Pristine Place

Boggart Hole Clough was absolutely pristine, and they had a lot of people to keep the grounds up. Everyone went parading up and down, and they had a beautiful tea-room there. It breaks your heart to see them now.

Ron Burrows

Skating

There was a roller-skating rink at Spotland Bridge. You borrowed the skates when you got there. They had instructors on and if you were a beginner and couldn't do very well they used to come and guide you round, and then they left you and went on to someone else. You could go skating in winter, at Hollingworth Lake and at the sewage works.

Jean Roberts

Tea Out

You could get a jug of tea at Carr Wood Tea Rooms. We used to get the bus to Norden and walk all around.

There was a nice café at the back of Hollingworth Lake. When I was courting it was revived, and we used to go and have our dinner there. During the war they used to have Sunday teas. They were very well attended; there was that little bit extra and long tables with everyone sitting around together.

The Group

An Easter fair at Hollingworth Lake.

Icicles on the old railings and gateway to Hollingworth Lake.

Fireworks at Bellevue

We used to go to the public firework displays on the lake at Bellevue. In November it would go on for about a month: there was a slope behind the lake and mock battles on what looked like boats on the lake. There was the speedway; the zoo and you'd take a picnic. It was accessible, you could get on the tram and go.

Alan Mills

The Grapes

There used to be a pub on Bull Brow, the Grapes, and we used to go past there. I said once to my mother, 'Those women in there, they sound to be having such a good time, can we go in?' 'Come on' she said, and pulled me away!

I remember going in there just after the war and I remember all these girls sitting round and they were drinking 'red biddy'. They drunk a lot of port and they used to put gin in those barrels so it used to come out red.

Sheila Jones, Alan Mills

A Drink at Home

Women didn't go into pubs in those days. You could go along to a pub in Belfield, take a jug along to the window and take it home. This was the 'jug and bottle department'.

I used to go down to the Weaver's on Ashton Road every Sunday with a jug so we could have a glass of ale with our Sunday dinner – I wasn't the only one making the trip, I can tell you!

Sheila Jones, Ronnie Kershaw

73

Friends on holiday.

The Blue Bell

One of the oldest pubs in Rochdale was Yates's Wine Lodge. It used to be called the Blue Bell. The bell was from the church and it was a blue colour. They segregated themselves: there was a tap, a snug and then a general public room, and later on there was a ladies' room as well before they opened them all up.

Alan Mills

Jokers!

Miners worked six inch seams and they'd egg this fellow on in the pub – this chap, they got him so excited they got him lying down on his side to show them this seam – and they were pulling his leg all the time. The other one was apple sauce, 'Rubbish, rubbish, who eats pork with apple sauce' and one fellow down in the Miner's Arms got his wife to make some to show them – they got up to all sorts of daft tricks.

Ronnie Kershaw

The Fair

Fairs and circuses used to come. My mother used to know the people, they were Mitchell's from Heywood and they owned the fairground at the cattle market. The oldest two sons used to do most of it and Mr Mitchell had his caravan just in the entrance against the wall by the Manchester Road. He always wore a bowler hat and tie and suit and if anyone were complaining they had to go to him to sort it out.

Kath's friends enjoying the beach.

There was a caterpillar ride, a moon rocket, the whip, and later there was a speedway ride. They arrived on flat cars, towed by a showman's traction-engine called *Lancashire Lad*. I used to ride down on my bike to watch them build the rides up. Then small stalls were set up, and sideshows wherever they could.

They used to stay a week and longer when we had 'holidays at home' in wartime.

Jim Barham

The Circus

I taught at Cronkeyshaw School and Billy Smart's Circus used to come to Cronkeyshaw Common. We liked it because their children used to come to our school and we used to get free tickets to the circus. They were well-to-do people and the animals were well looked after.

The elephants came by train and walked down Drake Street. I remember having to stop on Old Street, they were like a little chain, all linked trunk to tail.

There were quite a lot of trees on Cronkeyshaw Common and they used to tether the elephants to the trees. I suppose they were very peaceful elephants or they could have gone off with the trees! They used to put as many animals outside as they could to enjoy the sunshine.

Barbara Eldred, Kath Ward

Home by Eight

I used to have to be in by eight o'clock; my mum or dad would come out for me.

Anyway one evening I and this other girl were making off to the fair. I don't know how my dad knew, but he came after us and made me go back home.

Jean Roberts

The Good Old Days

I wouldn't want to go back to the 'good old days' but I wouldn't mind going back to being twenty-five again!

Ronnie Kershaw

CHAPTER 7

Church and Chapel

Baillie Street Methodist church.

Tin Tabernacle

Life seemed to rotate around the church. We went to Sunday school and we went to church. We had what we called the 'tin tabernacle' in New Moston and this was a corrugated shed. There was a very good vicar, the Revd Poyser Bullock who was a great one for drumming up money: he would talk to anyone and try to get money out of them because he wanted to build a new church and so he did. But it was the tin tabernacle when we were quite small and we thought it was a marvellous place, with a snooker-table in it. Do you remember Johnny King, the boxer – he used to go there to play billiards. We could go there and watch and he'd eventually come out and speak to us. He let us take his baby out for a walk in the pram.

When the new church was going up one of the builders slipped down on the roof and fell all the way off. We promptly hightailed it home to tell our mothers. It was not an auspicious start!

Ron Burrows

*Ron and his older brother in the church Lads'
Brigade during the 1930s.*

A Way of Life

It wasn't just the church, it was a total
environment.

Ron Burrows

Great Uncle's Catechism

Mother had an uncle – he had a tinsmith's
business – who was very religious. Every
Sunday they had to go to visit him and
they'd be sitting in his study, while he had
his velvet jacket on and a little cap, and he
used to question them on the bible. They
were frightened to death.

Ron Burrrows

'The Devil's Visiting Cards'

I was brought up on the straight and narrow.
My grandmother was very strict. On
Sundays you couldn't chop wood. As for
having beer in the house that wouldn't do at
all – it was 'the devil's visiting cards'.

They used to have these little parties
where they'd play whist, and there was a
café in Sudden where they had this whist
drive and offered the money to the church.
They wouldn't have it.

Alan Mills, Anon

Youth Club

We had a youth club and used to meet in the
parish rooms. We didn't often have
speakers, we used to sit around and gossip
more than anything, but as the war started
the older youth went away and left the
younger ones.

I was about sixteen, so the sixteen-year-
olds used to go down to the parish rooms
every time the sirens went and fire-watch
for the church. What they thought two
sixteen-year-olds could do with a big
church!

Barbara Eldred

The Methodists

At Baillie Street there was a big church and
that was the Methodist. It seemed to be
dead during the week, but it was next to the
public hall and all the activities were there.
There was a very good choir. They used to
get some very well-known singers – Isobel
Bailey – and the church was well-supported

by quite a lot of the mill-owning families, Duckworth's and Turner's were Methodists.

Jim Barham, Alan Mills

The Wesleyans

I used to go to Sunday school and we used to go to the primary class beneath the Wesleyan chapel – it's gone now. There's another case of how different they were.

We used to play badminton at St Edmund's and when the war started the hall was taken over, so I thought, 'There's a nice hall at the Sunday school', but no. It was used for sales of work and teas – men's teas at one and six a head with ham salads and things. Some churches used to welcome these dance parties and the like, but these Wesleyans wouldn't have it at all.

Of course in the earlier days, when there was no entertainment, if there was something made for you, you used to go to it.

Alan Mills

Fund Raising

They had sales of work, not money-making things really, but sheets and blankets, and they worked all through the winter to make things.

We used to have ours outside our church in the summer.

In the Sunday school they used to make kettle holders (the kettle was invariably on the hob and with iron handles the whole thing got very hot), and needle cases with a bit of flannel in the middle.

The Group

Mothers and children from Moore Street chapel on a visit in 1926 to the Moorland Home which they supported. Kath's family attended this chapel.

St Mary's Sunday School

Well I went, and still go, to St Mary's. There's a day-school where we had the Sunday school. There was a huge stage and curtains and all the lighting. We used to put on a lot of plays. I was never in them – I was always one of those putting make-up on – I was quite happy doing that. We used to do plays at Easter and Christmas. There used to be dances in the Sunday school where all the girls sat on one side and the boys sat on the other and looked across at each other.

Barbara Eldred

Sunday School Teacher

I was a Sunday school teacher. I had a group of fifteen-year-old lads. For instance, I took them up the tower of the church at great personal risk – apparently it was unsafe! The zoo vet, David Taylor, he was one of my pupils, and Tom Wakefield, the organist. I had this class for years – there were about fifteen in it.

Ronnie Kershaw

Participation

Ours can't have been a very good church or I wasn't that keen. I was always trying to get off into the industrial out yon where things were happening.

But there were one or two enterprising teachers: they used to set experiments up to explain the parables, but it didn't last very long, then it didn't hold us.

Jim Barham

Jean (far right) sang in St Edmund's church choir, pictured here around 1940.

Jean enjoying a St Edmund's church choir outing to Llandudno shortly before the war.

Sunday School Prizes

On Prize-giving Day we all used to be given books of parables and something like that, but now they're not, they're given Roald Dahl. Or the older ones have a book token. Oh yes, I've still got one or two of my prizes.

I think all the kids signed the pledge and their prizes were what I call uplifting novels, where good always triumphs!

The Group

St Edmund's Church

There were concert parties – the Mothers' Union used to get them together, apart from the choir. I'm the little one in the picture of one of these. There was the Boys' Brigade,

the Girls' Brigade, a band and Harry Simms, he wrote one or two of these things.

Jean Roberts

In the Pantomime

These were heady days – the youngsters did all the Christmas pantomimes. Everyone used to try to get selected; it was quite a feather in your cap to get selected for the panto! Of course I didn't realize at the time, there was a hierarchy at the top who really ran this dramatic society.

During the wartime, they were always getting me to be in the plays and as soon as I came back from the forces they were virtually waiting on the doorstep to get me back because they'd lost young people and after the war people didn't have the same interest in it. I remember there always had to be a fireman at the door when we put a show on, with his helmet and his axe – we thought this was marvellous.

Ron Burrows

An Individual Organist

There was one member of our church who used to play the organ, but he was a right funny character. If he got any pound notes and they hadn't been washed or anything and he got into a taxi he'd hold them out the window to get the air circulating before he put them in his pocket. He preferred sovereigns.

Alan Mills

Something for Everyone

Anyone who didn't go to church wasn't quite one of us. There was the Women's Voluntary Service and the Mothers' Union so everyone was involved, the vicar did parish visits and all the kids went to Sunday school.

Ron Burrows

Whit Friday Preparations

All the teachers at Sunday school, we used to make paper flowers, or tissue-paper flowers, and put them on these different banners to spell out 'God is Love' and 'Teach the Children'.

Barbara Eldred

Walking the Parish Bounds

The Catholics had to cover the whole town between two parishes. It was a tramp, bands leading the way and behind. We were in the middle, but they couldn't keep in time. They played different tunes and couldn't hear each other!

All the clergy came in their robes, and the two May queens shook hands – it was a great occasion.

Sheila Jones

Afterwards

Most of us didn't have to walk very far; the fields came quite close into town.

After the procession we went into the field, there was a pie and an orange, then we ran races – sack race and egg-and-spoon – and there was a side-stall selling sweets.

The bands stopped and played a while. If it was wet we had to go indoors, but it wasn't so enjoyable.

The Group

The parish church first floodlit in 1935.

St Edmund's Whit Walk.

Boys in tabards assembling outside the town hall during the Whit Walks.

Sheila and her brother Frank took part in this Sacred Heart Whit Walk, c. 1955.

Whit Friday, 1927.

Jean, aged seven, accompanying the banner along Clement Royd's Street towards St Edmund's.

Combined Church of England churches gather in the Town Hall Square at Whit. St Chad's choir and their choirmaster Mr Nuttall are in the foreground.

CHAPTER 8

During the War

Joan's father in charge of the ARP ambulance, outside Castlemere School in 1943.

A Dark Time

It was a darkish time for me, in our house, with the war. It was hard going.

It was a real upheaval, knocking families up in one way or another. I wouldn't like to go through it all again.

The Group

The Strength of the People

I can't recollect that I ever thought that we were going to lose the war.

I remember being on fire guard duty (in Plymouth) and the Yanks were guarding their own stuff and this particular fireman was talking about these raids there'd been recently in the area.

A soldier of the First World War: Uncle Ted was killed on the Somme in 1917. Here he is in Royal Artillery uniform, but Ronnie remembers him as the favourite uncle who showed him a curlew's nest.

He said in Britain there was something remarkable about all these raids – no one seemed to panic. The women were so brave; he was quite amazed at the strength of the people.

Alan Mills

A Holiday from School?

What I remember is the war breaking out. I thought about that more than anything because we didn't have to go to school, which was rather nice. But they didn't have enough shelter. We thought the first thing that ever happened we'd all be dead, and then it got as we did half days at school until they got these places for us to go.

Jean Roberts

Left Behind

When the war broke out, the school evacuated, but there were about half a dozen of us in our locality and we didn't evacuate. We had about six weeks' holiday and our parents got a bit annoyed about this!

Ron Burrows

The First Alert

I was in the bath when the alert went. I shot out and under the stairs where we had a cupboard – nothing on and rather wet – my mother was there. She was in the other room and we shot in together.

Barbara Eldred

Prisoners of War

Where Stakehill is now, at the time there were soldiers there, a prisoner of war camp, but they were mistaken for something else and bombed.

We used to run patrols round in case they were escaping. They used to exchange visits later with the older people, each year they'd come back or they'd go over to Germany. We seem to have been so relaxed in many ways yet they didn't escape.

Jean at nineteen in the ARP.

The Italians were let out to work on the farm near my gran's. We used to give the dots and dash victory signal as we walked past – we were awful to tease them.

The Group

The Anderson Shelter

Anderson shelters – you had to put them in your garden and I remember my father being furious because you had to dig this hole, then cover it with sods on top so it was just like a mound. We never went in.

We had ours all concreted and made very nice, but we stopped going after a while.

Anon, Ron Burrows

A Cosy Cellar

We used it when there might be bombs. We had a fire and used to have our baths down there, nice and hot, and we slept in there. It was lovely, I liked it much better than the other. It was all piles of wood. There were five of us and father had it all done you see, with these big planks to hold it up in case the house fell down. I never wanted to come up at all! There was a window with curtains for fresh air, we had a wireless down there and listened to Lord Haw-Haw. We were all in the same place.

Jean Roberts

A Morrison Shelter

Mr Johnson came to see our Mr Foster about 1941 to 1942 to ask them to make a Morrison shelter. These shelters were about eight feet long by three feet high and were made out of steel angle sheet and wire mesh. They were used as an air-raid shelter-cum-table.

Steel of any kind needed a requisition form from the Ministry of Supply. We did this, made the shelter, transported it to Mr Johnson's house in Southport and assembled it in one of the rooms.

Jim Barham

Official Provision

We were given a key to the street shelter, but it was never built!

Barbara Eldred

Blackout

It was really dark in the blackout, you had tissue-paper on your torches, and there were dimmers on the buses.

It was great for astronomy in those days! I walked into a gas light and had a great lump on my forehead.

The Group

Stirrup-Pumps

You had stirrup-pumps, a bucket of water and sand.

You could run up to an incendiary bomb as it fizzed and put a bag of sand on it. They were compulsory – you felt you were doing your bit.

Jim Barham

Jim in uniform,
Christmas 1944.

Fire Duty

Wherever you were when the war started you were on an ARP party. At weekends if you were set in an area with about three or four firms, there'd be twenty or so of you and five or six had to be on duty each weekend on the roof. You were there all day and all night like for a weekend. Most of the mills were going night and day. Also the poor apprentices in the engineering place had to do all that and go to night-school three nights a week. So you were working seven days a week and sleeping when you could. It was hard work for the first three to four years, then you got called up for your trouble.

Jim Barham

Bevin Boys

When I was eighteen I was called up. They thought they might get me off, they were doing Bevin Boys then. If your firm requested that you weren't called up, you'd join the Bevin Boys that were coal mining. They put in a request for me to stay as they were all old people getting on, but they didn't get me off.

Jim Barham

Parts for Tanks

We made gear wheels, blanks to be cut by Smith's up at Whitworth. They used to come and put teeth on 'em for tanks. We did that till Thursday, then on Friday we got everything ready for the weekend. By that time mills were working seven days a week, twenty-four hours a day making cloth and anything for the war. One part of the mill wouldn't be able to keep up with another part so what they did, they wanted this part isolating. So we had to put a clutch in where the shaft drove this part of the mill to disconnect this part from the other. That's what we were doing. We'd go in Saturday dinner-time and be working all night, all Sunday, until it was finished, ready to run and start up again Monday morning.

Jim Barham

Pursuit by Plane

I was a warden. I was pedalling down one night when the siren went off.

There were bright stars and this plane coming over Rochdale. I could swear it was following me. In the event it went over Knowl Hill.

Alan Mills

Manchester Bombed

My dad was just over the age group for going in the war, so he went onto the ambulance service. He stood in for first aid and passed all his exams so when they dropped the bombs on Manchester he were stationed there for about a fortnight, sorting everything out. I believe it was terrible.

Joan Thomson

Smog

When the war started that killed off a lot of social activity, what with blackout and fog – with all the mills going there was three times as much smoke.

Jim Barham

Fuel for the Fire

You burnt anything you could find.

'Nutty slack' was delivered. It was the left over after all the coal had been taken out. It was slow to burn, you had to put your hands round to get any heat out of them.

My dad used to put them together with cement and make them up into briquettes.

There was peat as well. We stored a pile of these in the garden and they're still there.

The Group

Rationing

When they started rationing we were coping with people who could register with us as we were the only grocer in the district. You got a meat ration for making your meat pies from the Ministry of Food.

When you were registering you had to give the figure – so much of butter a week. You'd put this down and on that they'd base the rations. It was fair.

Then they brought in things at odd times, for points, various things where there was a shortage.

Kath Ward, Alan Mills

The Sweet Ration

People wanted what they could have in the way of cakes. You had to ration them.

You know those toffee trays that you used to get – we had the sweet ration and to make sure everyone had what they wanted you had a tray and put six on with someone's name. You had to be very careful you didn't offend anyone.

Then of course that was Saturday mornings when they came for these – well, we were supposed to open at nine o'clock, and at eight o'clock they were rattling on the door, and you were still busy trying to get these cakes out, and the door handle was going like that.

Kath Ward

Queuing for an Orange

People would come, they all used to cling together, and they'd say, 'Oh, they've oranges at such-and-such a shop on Oldham Road' and I'd have to queue for one orange – you were only too pleased to get it.

This was more or less what kept my mother going because with working she was never there to get any of it.

Joan Thomson

The End of Rationing

With sweets you used to get all these points and count them and they'd give you a permit to buy so many points' worth of sweets. It went on till 1951. It was taken off suddenly and everyone went and bought up the shop! But Gibson's and

Porter's decided that week they'd have a holiday – they weren't going to give all their sweets to anyone!

The following week, there'd been such a rush on these sweets they put them back on rationing again. They were the only ones to have any sweets in the shop.

Alan Mills

Wartime Weddings

There were clothing coupons and people who were getting married got extra points for sheets and things.

For wedding-cakes someone would give their raisins up and so on. Icing was forbidden so some wedding-cakes were covered with a chocolate couverture.

Then you could have a sponge-cake with a fancy cardboard top to go on it. We had one of those: it was made to look like icing, but it had to go back again afterwards.

Sheila Jones, Jean Roberts

Stewed Beef and Carrots

You could go out to a restaurant provided you had the points. There was a set price – five shillings for a three-course meal. The idea was these big hotels couldn't live on the fat of the land at the expense of others.

They got over this by charging covers: when you sat down they'd promptly charge you three and six just for the privilege of going and eating in their place, so you paid eight shillings and sixpence. But if you went to the Civic Restaurant you could get a two-course meal there for one shilling. They'd do stewed beef and carrots, rice pudding, jam roly-poly.

Alan Mills

Bread-and-Butter Pudding?

I remember going to the Civic Restaurant one time. It was at the back of Oldham Road, near the Alhambra. They had some trays and were putting bread on them and some water and pressing it down and then they sprinkled it with a few sultanas. 'This is going to be bread-and-butter pudding.' They cooked this in the oven and poured some custard over it, watery custard!

Alan Mills

Ingenious Substitutes

Then there was snook – a tinned fish, pink and sloppy like salmon – it was the 'nutty slack' of fish! Then there was whale meat; you could make a steak and kidney pudding of that.

For fat in cakes they used liquid paraffin – not too much! I knew someone was scraping the grease off the lathes and using that as fat. She always had cake and no one could understand it. That was how she was doing it.

Sheila Jones, Jim Barham

Wonderful Concerts

Talking about Rochdale having some

**CHAMPNESS HALL,
ROCHDALE**
Monday, September 20th, 1943
at 6-45 p.m.

LOUIS COHEN

AND THE

LIVERPOOL
PHILHARMONIC
ORCHESTRA
Leader—HENRY HOLST

Solo Pianoforte—LOUIS KENTNER

This Concert has been organised in conjunction with the Council for the Encouragement of Music and the Arts.

PROGRAMME   SIXPENCE

Music by Schumann and Dvorak's New World Symphony *were performed at this concert in 1943.*

Fashion Corner was illuminated to celebrate VE Day.

culture then, during the war they dispersed all these orchestras, and in the Champness Hall we had some wonderful orchestral concerts and famous pianists like Myra Hess. We had more music then than before or since.

Anon

Full House

It was the hey-day of the cinema to some extent during the war. I can remember queuing up nearly every time in wartime. The sirens would sound, one or two used to get up and walk out, but we just stayed put. You got used to it.

Ron Burrows

Practising for the Band

Of course, all the men had got called up out of the Salvation Army band, so the girls got the trumpets. Our manageress was down in the cellar, practising, learning how to play the trumpet – honestly, there's nothing worse! I used to say, 'I'll just go to the cake shop' and I used to go out and you could hear her all over Yorkshire Street.

Joan Thomson

VE Day

I can remember VE Day because they got the lights on. Fashion Corner was all lit up with coloured lights and there was dancing on the Town Hall Square. People were

A military band marches in procession past Halfpenny's and the Stylo shoe shop.

walking up and down Drake Street and I was with a school friend and the American she later married. He said, 'It's just like Time Square.' And then you were dancing with people you didn't know.

Kath Ward

VJ Day

On VJ Day we were pea-picking. It was a holy day and me and three other girls went down to mass in the village and while we were there the priest said, 'I'll keep you the minimum length of time, because I'm sure you all want to be at home rejoicing with your families.' We asked what had happened and when we heard the Japanese had given in, I can remember dashing back up Parbold

Hill to the camp and telling everyone. They said, 'We know – the butcher's been.'

Sheila Jones

Companionship

I know it sounds a terrible thing to say, but the time during the war was one of the nicest times of my life. I had a lot of friends, and my friend had three girls from Guernsey to live with them. We had an allotment, the five of us, and we did all the vegetables for the two families. I was about sixteen and they were varying ages and we had a very happy time – but we didn't lose anybody.

Barbara Eldred

Rochdale Home Guard, photographed by Jean from her office window, at the corner of Fleece Street and Drake Street.

CHAPTER 9

Special Days

Kath's birthday party at Overt Street.

The Birthday Cake

I've got a photograph of about seven or eight of us – friends from school or neighbours, you know – in the backyard at Overt Street. Being brought up into a confectioner's I always had a birthday cake. My dad always made me one and I used to decide what colour I wanted.

We played party games like pass the parcel. There wasn't enough room for musical chairs.

Kath Ward

Birthdays

I don't remember much fuss being made of birthdays. We just wished somebody a happy birthday. I don't remember being showered with presents and birthday cards.

Sheila Jones

A Cherished Present

The main birthday I can remember, I was about eight or nine and I went up to my cousins. I'd got a new baby doll. I didn't have many dolls as I got mainly boy's presents – I had a train one year and things like that because I had mainly boy cousins – so I was very pleased with this baby doll. I took it up to my cousins and I don't think I'd been there more than half an hour and it was shattered completely. The only time I had a doll.

Barbara Eldred

Brothers and Sisters

A neighbour of ours had only boys and she got fed up waiting for a girl. She called me in one day and gave me this doll. It had real red hair and my brother gave it a shampoo and the wig came off.

Sheila Jones

Party Games

We had friends in and used to play games like guessing blindfold what was on the plate. People used to put horrible things on the plate to taste and put your finger in. A quarter of an orange or a squishy grape, a dragon's eyeball. Then there was putting the tail on the donkey and guessing who'd gone out of the room.

Pamela Hutchinson, Sheila Jones

Just the Thing for Little Lads

There were indoor fireworks, little volcanoes and serpents you lit and when it burnt it used to go along like a great big grey tail. It smelt horrible. You couldn't get away with it now – the whole room was full of smoke – just the thing for little lads to play with. Then we had a magic lantern with a little oil lamp and films. It used to take my dad about an hour to set it up and get it going and then it was over in a flash. He could never quite adjust the lamp properly to get the best picture, and it smelt horrible of course. It only came out once or twice a year. I've a feeling he had a Charlie Chaplin film.

Ron Burrows

More Games

We used to have a game of stations, little piles of tickets up and down the stairs. You all had a clue and you had to collect these tickets. There was a treasure-hunt with dried peas: the person who found the most won a prize, a bar of Fry's chocolate or a little pencil.

No birthday party was complete without jelly and blancmange.

The Group

A Conjuror

The last party I had, I'd be about twelve. Norman Evans came. His parents and my parents were friends and it was before he went into the theatre professionally. He brought his doll Jimmy, he was a ventriloquist in those days, and I don't think I appreciated it as much as I would do now! He did a few conjuring tricks, and took a penny out of my ear. I wondered how he managed it!

Anon

Home Music Making

The parties I remember were Sunday evenings when my uncle played the violin and my father played the piano and people came. We had all the popular songs of the day.

Ronnie Kershaw

Christmas Presents

At Christmas we always hung our stocking up. We'd maybe find an apple, orange and nuts.

I had books mainly, annuals.

The Group

A Wartime Tree

I remember during the war, and my mother said, 'We don't want to not have a tree this

Neighbours in Norden. The District Surveyor (before incorporation into the Borough of Rochdale) with his glamorous family.

year' and she went all around and finally came up with a little thing about that big [eighteen inches], a stick with no greenery on it, but we had our tree and we trimmed it up with some glass decorations.

Barbara Eldred

Tree with Candles

We had an artificial tree of wire and green raffia and at the end of each branch was a little metal cup and you put a candle in and lit it. Once it was all set up you were allowed to watch it for a few minutes and then it was quickly put out.

Ron Burrows

Decorations

We usually had our tree on the middle of the tea table on Christmas Day and then it was lit. We had some Chinese lanterns. My grandfather had been a sailor and they came from abroad.

We made paper chains from gummed strips and sticky paper and you could use flour and water paste – there was no Sellotape.

Kath Ward

Holly and Mistletoe

We always had holly and mistletoe on the door and over the light, and an ornament of a bird in spun glass with a tail.

Anon

Family Celebrations

On Christmas Day it was just your immediate family. It was Boxing Day when you went out for the family party. In our families it degenerated into a whist drive for the adults while the kids all played in another room under the eye of my grandmother. She was a dab hand with the money but she was illiterate and couldn't play at the whist drive so she used to sit there keeping an eye on the kids.

Ron Burrows

Preparations

We made our own mincemeat of course and the cake was started in November.

Then for the pudding you wrapped threepenny bits in grease-proof paper.

The Group

Guy Fawkes

We used to go to a party on the Fifth of November. Someone would say, 'I'll do the bonfire this year' and we cooked potatoes in the fire but they burnt to a cinder!

We were going to one once and my father had this guy over his shoulder and we were stopped by a policeman who said, 'What's the matter with this man?'

My dad started laughing and the policeman didn't like it; he threw this thing down on the ground and of course it was just stuffed!

Ron Burrows

Boys dressed as the Dionne quintuplets as part of a Rose Queen procession during the 1930s.

The Carnival

There was the carnival. It used to be midsummer, before the war. Every notable firm, Duckworth's, Pioneer's, coal merchants, all had floats.

They collected for charity. The men held a sheet up between poles and people threw money down into it. There were entertainers in the street and clowns.

The Group

The Rushcart Revived – Again

The Rushcart was a revival about 1906, redone from a study of customs. My father was one of the people who pulled it.

The rushes came from Lobden, not the big bulrushes. It was revived again after the second war, so now it's a copy of the 1900s. It may not be traditional – the rushes could be merely piled on a cart and taken to church.

I remember Little Joss on the Rushcart. He was a First World War veteran who'd lost both his legs.

Ronnie Kershaw, Sheila Jones

The New Year

At New Year they used to come round with black faces and brushes, but ordinary clothes. They came in and never said a word, they had a sweep and you gave them something. They were local lads just collecting money for themselves.

Jean Roberts

Preparing the Maypole

Maypole Day is the first day in May, but it doesn't start then. It starts long before that. Weeks before, little girls get together in groups for you need six, five to dance around the maypole and one to be the May queen, who is usually the smallest. The girls saved their pennies for weeks for we needed ribbon and crêpe paper, two hoops which we got from the greengrocer and we borrowed a brush stale from one of our mothers.

The week before May Day was very busy for the girls. After school they had to practise the songs and they had to go to the shops to buy two yards of ribbon, and all the colours had to be different of course. There was often arguing as two of the girls often wanted the same colour.

The girls would cut the crêpe paper in strips and wrap them round the pole. Someone's dad would bind the hoops together to form a circle. When the hoops were in place they would be wrapped in crêpe paper and tinsel and baubles. The exciting part was nailing the ribbons to the pole: the maypole was now ready and it was looked at with pride, hoping that your maypole was better than the one in the next street.

E. Seddon

Left Out

I originate from Stacksteads, near Bacup. We would stop on every street and sing and dance and someone would collect pennies for us. It was the traditional song of 'Can you dance the polka' and the queen would stand up singing 'I'm the queen, etc.' (I never got to be queen) On one occasion we danced from our school, meeting all other schools in Bacup Park where there was a massive

A patriotic maypole at Norden.

The end of a perfect day: Kath and her friends on the field in 1927 after their Whit Walk.

maypole. It was lovely, the ribbons all plaited as we danced. The weather always seemed to be sunny. When I was seven I danced all day, but when they dished up the money, I'm afraid I got left out. I have never forgotten.

J. Hall

The Boy's Part

I remember taking part in the maypole dance when I was a small boy. The girls used to dress up and do the dancing and the boy's job was to carry the maypole and a little stool for the queen to sit on from one venue to another. The boys had to do the collecting while the girls were dancing. We used to perform outside the local mills, especially if it was pay-day, when the workpeople were coming out. I remember the last few lines of the song 'Goodbye dear friends, etc.' were sung to the tune of 'For he's a jolly good fellow'.

H. Wolfenden

Supplying the Hoops

I was brought up near the Birches Hotel, Whitworth. There were seven cottages containing nineteen children. The first Saturday in May the older girls would make the maypole. It was a broom handle with two hoops off a butter barrel supplied by my dad who worked in Grandad's shop, McDonnell's in Yorkshire Street. They would cover them in coloured paper and attach coloured ribbons which the dancers entwined. The May queen, usually the youngest girl, sat on a stool and held the pole (rather tricky).

M. Cairns

Good Times

I am eighty-five but still remember the good times in May. The first Saturday in May we used to have a carnival, starting from the town hall, up Manchester Road, along Drake Street and back to the town hall, with a dance at night in the town hall. We would go round to lots of streets, singing and dancing and collecting money for the hospitals. I remember it well, the song and dances are still in my memory.

E. Halliday

A Labour of Love

My mother always provided the lace curtain for the queen's long white train, held in place by a ring of bright flowers. She sat on a little stool and held the bottom of the brush handle while the dancers held a long length of the ribbons. They skipped once round and then back again (so the ribbons didn't get wrapped round the pole) and as they skipped they sang. I can remember being May queen twice when I was a child and lived on Ashfield Road. I was eleven years old when we moved to the top of Yorkshire Street and St James' church, and I never saw the maypole danced in that area. Thinking back, I suppose a keen eye would find many faults but we put our hearts and soul into that maypole and to us it was a labour of love and perfection.

V. Wilson

The visit of King George VI and Queen Elizabeth, now the Queen Mother, to Rochdale in 1938.

CHAPTER 10
A Walk Around Town

A view over the town with Kelsall and Kemp's mill chimney on the left and the Hippodrome on the right.

This chapter is something different. Because our experience was rooted in the locality, the details of topography seem especially important. Perhaps change was there throughout, but to many it seemed to be encapsulated in the physical change of Rochdale.

New ideas in housing, transport and town planning, alongside changes in employment shortly after the war led to the removal of long-established landmarks. It was not roads that were re-routed, it was people. The ring road swinging round the west and north of the town formed a barrier to be breached. Simply, as buildings looked different, things felt different.

The bus station moved, then the market, the cinemas went, the plethora of individual shops reduced. Although this was not one overnight change, we could look back from the 1950s and say that a decade earlier, or two or three, things looked much the same; while looking forward in the same way that sense of familiarity has gone and instead 'survivals' are identified.

So what we have done here is to take a trip around the town centre, perhaps a Saturday shopping expedition. It is a leisurely stroll and Kath and Alan would like you to accompany us. The pictures chart the changes that will soon follow.

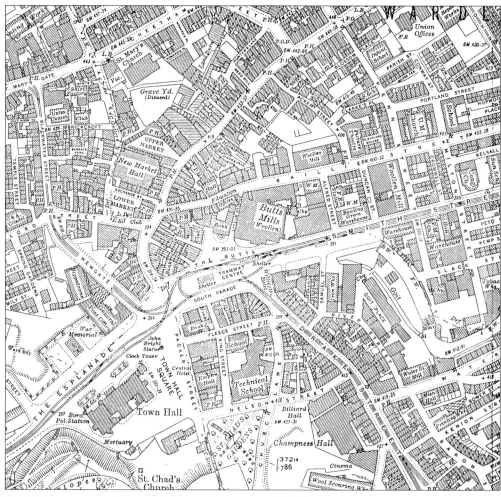

Rochdale town centre from an Ordnance Survey map of 1930.

The Walk

We're just arriving in town and thinking of going into the Walk.

We'll go into Porter's first and choose a box of Clifton's chocolates, they're a bit different, and what about a few twopenny bars of chocolate? There are 140 varieties to choose from – Turkish delight, fruit and nut, some fruit creams and peppermints.

Duckworth's is on our left. 'The Harrods of Rochdale' started here. This was the main grocery store, then they had a number of branches. It was double-fronted with various coffees and cheeses set out; not particularly expensive. My great-grandfather came from Stratford-on-Avon [*Kath*]. He was a baker and became Head Baker at Duckworth's, on Oldham Road where it backs onto the canal by Halfpenny Bridge. They were part of the town and one of them became mayor of Rochdale. I went from school to Mrs Mary

The Red Lion on Lord Street viewed from Newgate near the Hippodrome.

Duckworth's funeral at Baillie Street church.

Lord Street

We've crossed Yorkshire Street into Lord Street. The Provident Store – well, it wasn't the Provident Co-op any more, but we had two Co-ops in Rochdale, the Provident and the Pioneer's, and eventually the Provident dissolved and the Pioneer's took it all over. This store had furnishing, clothes, shoes. We often went to dances on the top floor – someone would rent it for a special party.

Now we're coming onto Newgate, past the Coffee House on the corner. Let's go back up Lord Street. There's Butterworth's tobacconists and a pawn shop; that was an old building. At one time there was a treadmill there; you could see the old gear at the top.

Toad Lane

The Old Clock Face pub. That was an old place. They say when the Jacobites came, one of them married a barmaid there and set up as a whitesmith. Hamilton's were in the tin business for a long time.

We've turned the corner now and here's Irlam's tripe shop (we'll come to their restaurant when we go up Fleece Street). We go past the Brickyard (Brickcroft) where you can get boots and outdoor clothes, then here's the original Co-op and we've come up to St Mary's Gate. This hardware shop sells everything!

Blackwater Street, looking towards St Mary's Gate with the Unitarian church on the right.

The Norden bus going up Blackwater Street.

That's far enough. Let's turn round and go back down, past St Mary's Vicarage. There's the entrance into the Baum through the old graveyard. We used to go down into Yorkshire Street that way when we came down from Greenhill. Another Pioneer's for electrical goods and another hardware shop, and here we are at the market.

The Market

This is the new building (in the 1930s) after the fire. There used to be a big open market at the bottom, but everything was burnt out, even the two pubs. The water-mains in Toad Lane were all furred up so the firemen could only get a trickle out; it was hard to get any pressure.

The market was much better laid out than the present one. You could walk through from Yorkshire Street to Toad Lane and there was the outside market at the back. There were the specialist shops for chicken, fish, eggs and the butcher's – it was like a little apse as it went round, all very handy.

There's a particularly good cheese stall run by two sisters called Jones. They sell Lancashire cheese from the real farm places, and Cheshire cheese and eggs. Their brother has the chicken side of the farm at Church, near Oswaldtwistle, and he has the stall selling chickens. The chickens have always been very healthy, fed just the way his father did when he started about 1910.

Home-made toffee on this stall and here's the popular biscuit stall where you choose them from the tins and have them weighed out.

Newgate looking up Blackwater Street with the Citadel on the left. Pilkington's furnishers, next door to the Duke of Wellington pub, has just gone.

Cheetham Street, with St Mary's church on the left, looking towards the Co-op head office on the right.

We can come out of Lord Street here, by the Pioneer's photographers, then there's the wool shop. You see the plaque on the wall? That's for the first charter for Rochdale Market. The little gap here was planned as an arcade, but the building was interrupted by the war and the little shops were never finished.

Yorkshire Street

We'll go up on the left as far as Cheetham Street. Just here there's the old building that used to do as a town hall, then Elwood's silk shop, Samuel's jewellers, and the second entrance up to the open market. Boots chemist is on the corner, Freeman Hardy Willis for shoes, and Woolworth's. We could go into Woolworth's – it's sixpence for everything!

Here's the Maypole, with their own brands of tea and margarine, they pat the butter and stamp it with a rose or a contented cow, not a maypole, though. Montague Burton's sells fifty-shilling suits. You can have one made up in about a week.

Dunn's the hatters are a little cut above the rest with wooden show-cases and nice drawers. If you buy a bowler-hat they'll put it on a form, stretch it to a precise fit, brush and polish it, so that it's presented to you without a finger-mark on it. They're just for gents' hats, with a few ties and scarves.

Turner's was where my grandmother used to go for fabrics and haberdashery; she was a dressmaker [Kath]. There was always a chair for you to sit down, and when you paid the assistant she put the money in a canister and away it whizzed and came back receipted.

The Scotch Woolshop is along here, and more clothes shops, Wolfenden's and Erroll's outfitters and Kerr's general drapers. It's quite a walk, but there's the underground toilets at the corner of Cheetham Street!

We're passing Preston's, jewellers and fancy goods, Curry's radio and cycle shop. Samuel William's is a huge place full of pots, dinner plates stacked up in piles; the classic pot shop. Bailey's higher up do cut glass and vases. Wilson Brothers' paint shop must serve all the decorators in town with their pigments. The boxes are full of different colours and the place is colourful from all the dust. Coming back down now, we must pass half a dozen pubs along the way.

The Keen Spot specializes in curtain material; they're a mill outlet. Shorrock & Shorrock's have their radio branch here, and sell pianos from their Drake Street shop. Liddell & Taylor's are second-hand dealers in rather good clothing. With an estate, if someone had died the assistant would go round and clear out the wardrobe. They could be brand-new clothes. They kept a list of people and their sizes so they could

Yorkshire Street.

contact them if they had something coming in to suit them. They did very well – you could get a pair of socks, umbrellas, walking-sticks, sports clothes; they didn't go out of fashion. Mr Taylor and his assistant retired about twenty years ago.

The register office is along here, and there's a sub post office for the Yorkshire Street area. Other offices too, the Chamber of Commerce for export licenses and that sort of thing, a typing and duplicating bureau, some estate agents. There's the Crown wallpaper place, and after the White Lion Hotel it's Harrow's ladies' and gents' outfitters. They treat you as an individual; you see the person in charge, they're particular about getting the right thing and tell you if it suits you or not!

We've a choice of printers: Howarth's do magazines for businesses, catalogues for factories, and if anyone is publishing a book they could handle it, while Wrigley's do stationery and books for bookkeeping.

After the Home and Colonial grocers there's Marks and Spencer's, but all clothes before they digressed into food. The Puff Puff is the best place for cigarettes (after the war he seemed to get a good supply and everyone was going to the Puff Puff). Plenty to choose from here: butcher's, jeweller's, dry-cleaner's. The Direct Raincoat Company have a place on Drake Street as well. The firm makes them in Manchester and you can get a light raincoat for a couple of guineas or something like that. The Lancashire and Cheshire Rubber Company will keep you dry too, with rubber boots and rubber mackintoshes.

Blackwater Street, 1945.

Blackwater Street, 1945.

Near Baillie Street is J.J. Thomas the chemist. Mr Thomas and his son lived next door to us [*Alan*] and Harold was a keen fisherman – he'd rather fish than work in the shop! They had a shop in Drake Street too at the Champness Hall, with those jars of coloured liquid, reds and greens and blues, part of the decoration of the shop where the windows were blocked off by the backdrop. There's the Co-op confectioner's and butcher's and a small Littlewood's. The counters are open in corridors down the shop so you can pick things out and pass them to the assistant where she's boxed in by all these trays, rather like Woolworth's really.

Redman's is the best for bacon and some other groceries too. If we go into The Bun for coffee we can walk through and come out in the sweet-shop in Newgate. Senior's was quite a big place which used to be in two parts for gents and ladies; we went there for school uniform.

The Butts

We can go back through the Walk now and into The Butts. The bank on the corner is Williams Deacon's and if you look in the window of Montague Burton's you'll see the two suits. All the same price, the 'ordinary' and the 'great man' – the same size as Cyril Smith!

Let's cross over South Parade where the trams go one way round the island and then we'll be ready to walk up Drake Street.

The Esplanade with the No. 86 tram passing the town hall.

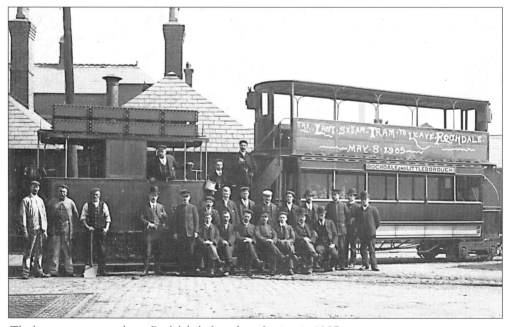

The last steam tram to leave Rochdale before electrification in 1905.

The last steam tram to leave Littleborough for Rochdale in 1905.

The first electric trams ran from Dane Street to the cemetery.

The Esplanade in 1932 with the art gallery, built in 1912, on the left.

Drake Street

While I was growing up, Drake Street was the high-class part with the better shops –there used to be some beautiful shops [*Kath*].

Pass the Wellington Hotel and the Rochdale Electric Company and here's Orrell's furnishers. Mr and Mrs Abrahams run the shop, I think she was an Orrell. You can get something just a little bit different to what you can find in the bigger shops. The Rochdale Rubber Company specialize in wellington boots. But if you want a costume for a special occasion, you must go into Eunice Fletcher's for ladies' gowns and further up the street for the milliner's.

The Savoy Café is a pretty popular rendezvous, morning coffee or a three-course lunch with waitress service. The councillors used to use the smoke-room at the back. In those days the councillors weren't paid and we used to get people from various offices who would come in, have a coffee and chew over what was going on in the town hall. They'd decide what to do, go back to the town hall to vote, and all the business had been done in the café in their own leisure time.

Sugden's was left to two sisters called Hardcastle who were Miss Sugden's assistants. It was a cosmetics shop and they were homely people for such a glamorous place. Cartwright's sells ladies' blouses; it's a little shop with a window on either side and a show-case down the middle so if we go in we'll be half-way into the shop before reaching the door. Singer Sewing Machines are just along here too.

Now if we had brought a bottle, we could go into the Empire Wine Store and they'd fill it up with sherry. Those two barrels on the back wall with a tap are imitation – nothing behind – just so that it looks as though it's coming out of a great sherry barrel!

We'll pass the photographer's and the ready-made clothing shop – all hanging up

The Esplanade.

Broadway around 1935, with Burton's on the right.

ready, a bit unusual, and then our only travel agent's, Thomas Cook's.

Now we've reached the Fashion Corner (Rochdale Pioneer's Society). It was like a department store; I've a great regard for the Fashion Corner, which sold children's things at Christmas [*Kath*]. My aunt was a war-widow from the First World War and always took me to the Fashion Corner to choose some wonderful present that Father Christmas would bring me. I got a little desk and chair, a collapsible table with a green top. I don't remember any

toyshops in the town centre, although there were stalls in the market, and a Dolls' Hospital.

Smith's is a wonderful greengrocer and fish shop – anyone who is anyone goes there. Four brothers and their sister each have their own jobs in the shop; the older brother delivers orders in a basket. The prawns come ready shelled in four-pound boxes. Just before the war they were selling lychees in their little shells. It was quite the thing to buy as we walked to school [*Kath*]. There was another fish shop

Town centre buses.

The Shakespeare pub on Bury Road. Brierley's mill and the telephone exchange, with the town hall behind.

The Esplanade, 1932.

in Blackwater Street where the lorry unloaded fish in boxes into a big opening in the wall for distribution to fish and chip shops [Alan]. They must have got their ice from the ice-making store in the old market. There was a refrigerated store there as well where you could take your stuff down, before people had their own refrigerators.

We'll go past the café, despite its renowned Eccles cakes, and come to the Yorkshire Penny Bank. When I went to school first, I used to take a penny on Monday and I had a bank-book. The teacher put the penny in and you used to watch the pennies and say 'Oh, I've got sixpence now'.

The Oldham Road branches off here. Budgen Allbury's is another old Rochdale firm for clothing. Cheap clothing comes from Hill's, bought with the Provident tickets. We've passed Ashton, Leach & Cumberbirch furniture shop and the old Masonic Hall. After the *Observer* offices and the corner of Great George Street is the Joyful News Bookshop. Clegg's started with religious books, so that's how it must have got the name. You would go there if you got a school prize.

Next comes Horrocks's bed-linen and gingham (the Preston firm). The Champness Hall is the Methodist church hall, and all the choirs use it for concerts.

There are the shops here too. In Dawson's Hardware, Mrs Dawson looks after the crockery and Mr Dawson has the hardware. Mr Dawson said 'I've just had someone in here wanting a kettle, but they didn't buy it. Don't they know it's raining now?' They were saving for a rainy day and found the kettle too expensive!

Now we're back to the lower part of Drake Street. Iveson's is a high-class furnisher's: lamps, pottery, wicker chairs, sofas, until you reach the top floor where all the carpets are laid out. They seem to do all the contracts for carpets. The optician's is run by Jack Etherington whose father had the chemist's shop next door. The Drake Hotel, you know, is named for a vicar, the same as the street.

Priestley's bag shop was set up by a jeweller from Manchester originally. Next door is the Universal Laundry, Ludlow's for radio, Ellison's wine and spirit merchants, a pet shop (in the 1950s) and of course Butterworth's jewellers. We mustn't miss Halfpenny's at the corner of Fleece Street. They sell lace collars and chokers to hide those wrinkles on your neck, or combinations, thick woolly vests, gloves and elastic.

We could go into Irlam's Restaurant. The shop on the ground floor sells tripe, elder and cow-heel and you can have some on a plate at one of the marble topped tables. This isn't the only tripe firm in Rochdale. They boil tripe on Primrose Street, off Spotland Road. You need to hold your nose as it goes in, but it comes out bleached and sparkling white!

Finally we're down to Howarth's on the corner of South Parade. It's like a department store full of separate rooms for dresses, corsets, accessories, hairdressing. It's called the Toggery. Now there's just the tobacconist and Louis furrier's.

The End of the Tour

We're back now at the bus or tram stop. We didn't go in every shop, and certainly not in all the shoe shops and outfitter's. But we didn't need to go into Manchester as we found everything we needed on either Drake Street or Yorkshire Street, and plenty of fresh food in the market.

You may recall these shops and others from the 1930s to the 1950s. Kath, Alan and myself hope you enjoyed going into town with us.

A view over the Orchard looking towards the town centre.

CHAPTER 11

Our Chosen Memories

Kath's uncle on a day's outing on the moors in the mid-1930s.

The Procession

One of my lasting memories is of a birthday party when the children and parents of the family came for tea. Mother had made a birthday cake. An older cousin by seven years had all the younger ones dressed as nursery rhyme characters and we walked in procession round the street ringing a bell. Most unfortunately an elderly man came out and asked us to stop ringing the bell as his wife was ill. So ended the procession.

Anon

The Dungeons

At the age of three and a half years I and my family moved into a new council house in Belfield. Immediately opposite, beyond a field, were the wild grounds of Belfield Hall demolished a few years previously. The girl next door said, 'Come on, I'll take you down the dungeons.' With knees knocking I went down a flight of steps into the earth but I saw no chained skeletons or drinking vessels. We emerged safely. Some busybody, or so we dubbed them, wrote to the council 'Did they know that children had access to

On holiday: Blackpool cliffs in 1934.

the cellars of the old hall?' The next day they were filled in.

Sheila Jones

Uncle has a Bath!

An amusing incident was when I was a child, we lived in a small house with very steep stairs.

One evening my uncle was going upstairs with a glass of water in each hand. Getting to the top the stair turned with very narrow treads.

He slipped and had to hold on to the tumbler and fall backwards. On each step his elbow jolted the water out of the tumbler. On arriving at the bottom he was very wet indeed.

Alan Mills

Visiting

I remember weekends at Auntie Betty's and Uncle Tom's cottage at Blackstone Edge. There was a spring outside for water, collected by jug and pail, and water ran into a bath. Someone once dropped Cousin Alan in the water.

Behind the cottage was a number of small lodges (originally there was a mill there) and the connecting channels had planks over them. I loved being taken round them; unfortunately Dad was always volunteered for the job.

We had to go to Littleborough by train and it was a long haul up Blackstone Old Road.

Anon

First Science Lesson

A day to remember was my first day at Greenhill Municipal High School for Girls. I started in October 1937 immediately after half-term and the first lesson that morning was a science lesson, the teacher being Miss Adcock. There were Bunsen burners at the end of the tables and litmus-paper and complicated charts on the walls and it felt like another world. At mid-morning break we crossed the asphalt playground to the dining-hall and had a small bottle of milk with a straw sticking out. I remember the milk was very watery. The milk cost twopence halfpenny for the week and you could have school dinners for two shillings a week.

Pamela Hutchinson

The Allotment

The time I recall was during the war when my friend Margaret's mother and father took one of the Guernsey girls as an evacuee. They found that she had two sisters and so they took all three. Margaret and I were twelve, the Guernsey girls were Betty (fourteen), Peggy (twelve) and Pat (ten). I was an only child and

Jim enjoyed the concert party at St Anne's.

Looking back: Halifax Road.

Stone cleaning and modernization: the corner of Oldham Road and William Henry Street in 1979.

thoroughly enjoyed all we did together. The best thing was that we got an allotment and grew all the vegetables for them and for three in my family all through the war. We used to walk from Spotland Road carrying our tools to Redbrook about every evening after school.

Barbara Eldred

An Exciting Journey

Before the Second World War our summer holidays were usually spent at resorts not too far away such as Blackpool or Hoylake, Grange-over-Sands or Colwyn Bay. In 1938 my parents decided we would go to Babbacombe in Devon. This required a lot of planning and the dispatch of a large trunk of clothes etc. as 'luggage in advance' by rail. The journey itself was very exciting for my brother and I (I was eleven and he was twelve) as this was a rail journey through the night. As we prepared to leave home a violent thunderstorm started and my parents wondered how to get us to the station in Manchester. Our neighbour came to the rescue and took us in his car. I think this may have been my first car ride. The train set off and for several hours the journey was accompanied by thunder and lightning. The two week holiday was a real adventure with coach trips to Land's End, Princetown (to see the prison) and lashings of Devonshire cream. The country was then very unspoiled, so different to today. The thunderstorm struck a chord, for many years later I went on my honeymoon to Babbacombe, the night of the Lynton/Lynmouth disaster.

Ron Burrows

As others see us? Rochdale's high rise skyline.

National and Local Events

I remember the visit of George V to Lancashire in 1913. I was in bed with measles and so I got up and hung our Union Jack out of the window. In 1925 it was the Jubilee. During the General Strike [1926] I had to walk from Healey to the secondary school. I won a competition in the *Guardian* and got a year's free subscription and so have taken the *Guardian* ever since. I also took my first trip abroad to Belgium with a school party.

Ronnie Kershaw

Let's go in a Taxi

The best thing I did must have been about 1937. We as a family used to go on the train from Wardleworth station to St Anne's on Sea for our holidays each year. This was a bit of a toil so out of the blue one day my grandad said, 'Let's go in a taxi' which would cost the earth.

So my dad booked the taxi which was a large old Austin of the funeral variety which we all fitted into. It was a man called Lance Atkinson and it cost three pounds ten there and back. This was never heard of in this time and I was thrilled to bits to be sitting in this all the way to St Anne's and back.

Jim Barham

And Finally

I don't believe in looking back.

Anon